Out of the Classroom and into the World

How to Transform Catholic Education

Praise for
Out of the Classroom and into the World

"It is with great pleasure that I see Roy Peachey taking up the challenges laid down by Stratford Caldecott in his ground-breaking work on education: formulating practical proposals for improving Catholic education, whilst maintaining a cultural breadth that I know Strat would have appreciated."—LÉONIE CALDECOTT, editor of the UK/Eire edition of *Magnificat*, UK editor of *Humanum*, and co-director of *Second Spring*

"Roy Peachey offers an incisive analysis of the commodification of knowledge, the utilitarian dominance of targets, and the scientism that has crept even into Catholic schools, and calls for a radical transformation of experience in a renewed Catholic vision of education as saint-making. He restores to parents their agency as their children's primary educators, and suggests some concrete ways in which this can be achieved. Philosophically sophisticated yet down-to-earth, this bold call to action should be read by all who care about the formation and welfare of children."—ALISON MILBANK, Associate Professor of Literature and Theology, University of Nottingham

"In *Out of the Classroom and into the World*, Roy Peachey makes an important contribution to helping Catholic parents, teachers, schools, and pastors take back ownership of Catholic education. For too long, Catholic educators have followed closely in the paths of their secular counterparts. Inspired by Stratford Caldecott's illuminating works on classical liberal arts education, Peachey successfully draws on the Catholic intellectual tradition, insights into today's challenges and opportunities, and his own long experience as a teacher and parent to provide learned and concrete insights into faith, human nature, teaching, and learning. Peachey's book will give

English-speaking educators firm starting points for considering how the wisdom of the Church can transform their work with students into joy-filled experiences of serious and fruitful learning."—ANDREW SEELEY, Executive Director of the Institute for Catholic Liberal Education and Tutor at Thomas Aquinas College, CA

"This is an important book for Catholic educators everywhere. Building on the solid foundation of parents' role as first educators, Roy Peachey traces out an attractive vision of what Catholic education could be, while remaining clear-sighted about the particular challenges—such as scientism and 'presentism'—now faced by those who are serious about changing contemporary culture. One of the most appealing aspects of the book is its breadth: it is so refreshing to read an account of Catholic education that has regard for both the intellect and will of the student! I very much hope that *Out of the Classroom and into the World* will be read widely and will live up to its title—making its influence felt beyond the classroom."—ROBERT TEAGUE, Headmaster, The Cedars School, Croydon

"For those homeschooling parents, like myself, whose educational philosophy is best expressed by the work of Stratford Caldecott, this is the book we've been waiting for. Roy Peachey takes the next step on behalf of Caldecott, not only identifying the complications and root causes of our current maladies, but also helping us to see in tangible ways how we can live out this vision and mandate of our faith in the domestic church, in our homeschools, and in our parochial schools. Just as Caldecott's books inspired a movement to bring beauty back into education, it is my hope as a parent and a Catholic that Peachey's book will be an inspiration in the ongoing transformation of Catholic education in the twenty-first century."—ANDREA KIRK ASSAF, creator of The Kirkos Caravan Cottage School

"Witty, personal, and authoritative, this beautifully written and deeply learned book makes fresh the timeless lessons of a Catholic education and gives a much-needed reminder to Catholic schools and colleges of what they are about. It will be welcomed by teachers, parents, and students alike as a vision of what they really desire when they go to school, or open a book."—ANDRÉ GUSHURST-MOORE, Second Master, Worth School

"Roy Peachey demonstrates a keen appreciation of and commitment to the central principle of Catholic education: that parents are the primary educators of their children. He deploys a wide range of scholarship, both ancient and recent, to reflect on the vocation of Catholic educators and schools to walk in loving accompaniment with parents in their educational endeavor and mission."—CHARLOTTE AVERY, Headmistress, St. Mary's School, Cambridge

ROY PEACHEY

OUT *of the* CLASSROOM *and into* the WORLD

How to Transform Catholic Education

⊕

Foreword by
Michael Hanby

First published
by Second Spring 2018
www.secondspring.co.uk
an imprint of Angelico Press
© Roy Peachey 2018
Foreword © Michael Hanby 2018

For information, address:
Angelico Press
169 Monitor St.
Brooklyn, NY 11222
angelicopress.com

978-1-62138-394-9 (pbk)
978-1-62138-395-6 (cloth)
978-1-62138-396-3 (ebook)

Cover design: Michael Schrauzer

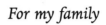

For my family

CONTENTS

Part One: Foundations

Part Four: Reflection

Acknowledgments

I am grateful for the help I have received from many people while writing this book. In particular, I would like to thank Ruth Ashfield for reading and commenting on an early draft of the first chapters, Léonie Caldecott for her support, and Audrey Donnithorne for her advice and encouragement. I would also like to thank Fr Gerry Devlin and Robert Teague, with whom I have had many fascinating discussions about Catholic education, John Riess for his wonderful work at Angelico Press, and Alice Gunther for her editorial input. I must also acknowledge the debt I owe to the late Stratford Caldecott, whose books and kind words set me off on the path that would eventually lead to the writing of this book. Above all, I want to thank my wonderful family for their love, patience, and tolerance. This book is dedicated to them.

Foreword

by
Michael Hanby

NEARLY EVERYONE AGREES these days that education is in
crisis, though unsurprisingly, the consensus ends there. A people
who can no longer agree on what a human being is—and education in the modern West is largely constituted by its refusal to
entertain this question—will be unable to agree on what education is and whom it is for. This makes contemporary education a
bit like building a house beginning with the second floor. Fash-
ionable ideas and techniques for "fixing" education, from aggres-
sive STEM education to providing each child with an iPad, are
stacked one on top of another without foundation. Few people—
least of all, it seems, the professional educators proffering these
techniques—pause to ask what education is. This is a philosophical, rather than a technical, question, which involves deep judgments about the nature of the human person and the meaning of
history. Consequently, most of these efforts merely treat the
symptoms with more of the disease.

This thoughtlessness is a symptom of the great disease of contemporary education—its *secularity*: the assumption that it
makes no difference to education whether we are children
known and loved into being by God or are merely accidental col-
lections of matter thrown up by meaningless material processes.
The attitude reflects a radical transformation in what it means to
think—the reduction of contemplative reason to pragmatic and
technical thought—as well as a utilitarian concept of education as
a kind of vocational training preparing young people for the
workforce. This, however, is ultimately to confuse education
with ignorance, for one cannot banish God from the curriculum
without losing much else besides. Banish God from the curriculum, and the great works of art, philosophy, and literature

become indecipherable symbols of a vanished past. Children become strangers to their own cultural and religious inheritance, prisoners, as Roy Peachey writes, of a kind of "presentism." The great questions that once animated Western culture—Who is God? Who am I? What is the good life?—not only cease to be answerable, they cease to be asked. Children, then, are given no great proposal, nothing beautiful or noble worthy of their love, and little to hope for beyond a life of comfort. They do not really learn how to read or how to think, and, worse still, they often become listless about their own educations. For children learn what we teach them, that education is merely a means to a practical end, and if that end can be achieved more efficiently in some other way—for instance, by cheating—so much the better. Utilitarian education thus ends up failing even by its own meager standards.

The renewal of education depends, therefore, upon the renewal of *Catholic* education. Yet all too often, Catholics have been unwitting accomplices in this reduction of the educational enterprise. Catholic parents, under pressure from our efficiency-driven capitalist culture, have largely succumbed to the modern view of education as a kind of career for children, administered by experts in possession of the latest technique or credentialed in "education science." Catholic schools, facing enormous social pressures of their own from universities and the standardized test industry, and often overwhelmed by the sociological services they are asked to perform, have largely acquiesced to the secular vision of education. They have submitted themselves to the same standards, adopted the same curricula, and employed teachers and administrators from the same schools of education that propagate the secular vision. This massive failure to pass on the faith, which now spans two or three generations, is evidence for a conclusion we ought to have understood intuitively. Merely adding "service learning" or religion class to a curriculum otherwise indistinguishable from its secular counterparts exacerbates the separation of faith and life, reinforcing the assumption of our secular and scientistic culture that religion and morality have little to do with *reality*.

There is no one in recent times who has done more to inspire the much-needed renewal in Catholic education than Stratford Caldecott, a friend and a gentleman in every sense of the word, who was taken from us much too early in 2014. Stratford's philosophy of education was as unique as he was, defying the usual categories. His approach was neither romantic nor classical, though it contained romantic and classical elements. It was certainly not utilitarian, though as an artist and a lover of art, he had a deep appreciation for all kinds of practical knowledge. He sought rather to put the child at the center of education, which meant protecting and cultivating the child-like love and wonder through which he himself saw the world. For Stratford's life was a life of love—love for the beauty of God above all, but also for His Church and His creation. Stratford saw this beauty everywhere he looked: in the love that moves the sun and stars, in the numerical patterns of nature and music, in the work of human hands, and in the ordinary, practical things of everyday life. Like Plato, Stratford understood that true education is learning to love beauty. And he helped many along this road with his own beautiful life and work.

Roy Peachey is one of many to come under Stratford's inspiration. Peachey writes in the same gentle and irenic spirit as Stratford, and his own experiences as a father and a teacher give this book a knowing and humane tenor worthy of its inspiration. From this serene vantage, Peachey invokes the aid of a wide range of authorities, from Aquinas to Neil Postman, to offer an insightful cultural analysis—a keen diagnosis of the ills of contemporary secular and Catholic education and many practical suggestions for its improvement. There is much wisdom here and much that is beautiful in its own right. *Out of the Classroom and into the World* is thus both a fitting tribute to the memory of Stratford Caldecott and an important contribution to the renewal of Catholic education that he helped to inspire.

Prologue

A COUPLE OF YEARS before he died, Stratford Caldecott wrote a wonderful book called *Beauty in the Word: Rethinking the Foundations of Education*. In a sense, it completed the work he had begun on liberal education with *Beauty for Truth's Sake: On the Reenchantment of Education,* but, in another sense, it was only the beginning of a greater project, for he always wanted to complement his largely theoretical books with practical suggestions for teachers and parents. I never met Stratford, but we discussed some of his ideas by email, and he then kindly offered me the chance to give a talk at St Benet's Hall, Oxford as part of his colloquium on humanizing work. Sadly, he was too ill to attend, but I hope he might have approved of the suggestions I made for reinvigorating our schools that afternoon, even though I now realize how half-formed my ideas were at the time.

Over the next few years, I found myself returning to the theme of Catholic education in various ways and in different guises, but it was only when three different strands of my life came together that I realized I could respond fully to the task Stratford had set us in *Beauty in the Word*. First and foremost, I am a parent. And, as a parent, I am my children's first educator. This simple but beautiful truth takes us to the very heart of Catholic education. It is, we could argue, the basis on which all true education is built. But I am not simply a parent: I have also been a teacher for over twenty years, working in both secular and Catholic schools.

I have been teaching for a long time, but I am constantly reminded how much I still have to learn about the basics. This was particularly (and literally) brought home to me when we started to home educate our oldest daughter. The joys and challenges of home education have forced us to rethink everything we thought we knew about education, while also bringing us in contact with ideas, approaches and people we would otherwise have entirely missed out on.

I write this book, therefore, as a parent, a teacher, and a home educator. I write this book to develop the ideas of Stratford Caldecott into a practical vision for Catholic education today. But, above all, I write this book for our children, convinced that what we have to offer them as Catholics can transform their lives. I know from personal experience the many failings of our current educational system, both secular and Catholic, but this is not a book that focuses on problems and neglects solutions. We cannot shy away from the many impediments that have been placed in our path, but we should always remember that there is a path to be trodden, a path that can take us on the most wonderful of journeys. We need to take a clear-eyed look at the obstacles we find in our way, but only so that we can remove them or, at the very least, bypass them. So this is not a book that dwells on the difficulties: it is a book with a message of hope. Catholic education can transform our children, and we can transform Catholic education. I don't know what Stratford Caldecott would think of this book, but I am sure he would agree with that.

Introduction

The Best of Times: The Worst of Times

I GREW UP in Dickensian England. To be more accurate, I grew up on the outskirts of Charles Dickens' Rochester. My journey to school took me past the Norman castle in whose moat Dickens wanted to be buried and the cathedral that featured in *The Pickwick Papers* and *The Mystery of Edwin Drood*. On the way home, I walked down the High Street (past my favorite homage to the great author: the Little Dorrit Tattoo Parlor) and changed buses outside Eastgate House, in whose grounds could be seen the Swiss Chalet in which Dickens was writing on the day he died. But all this passed me by as a boy. I didn't know much about Dickens, and the little I knew made me decidedly suspicious because, though I hadn't read any of his books, I had experienced the Dickens Festival.

The centerpiece of this annual extravaganza was a train that steamed down from London, carrying strangers in elaborate Victorian dress. Emerging from Rochester's Dickensian station, they processed into the center of town, spreading light and Victorian cheer as they went. Which was all very well for the adults. The problem, as I saw it, was that Dickens didn't create too many glamorous roles for children. My part in the proceedings was to walk around with dirt on my face and no shoes or socks on my feet. To make matters worse, my trousers and shirt were both torn to add an air of authenticity to my chimney sweep's costume, though the main effect was to induce near hypothermia. English weather is unpredictable at the best of times, and walking around as a shoeless chimney sweep with gaping holes in your clothes isn't adequate preparation for any festival at any time of the year.

So, despite being educated in Rochester, I did not appreciate the joy that Dickens can bring until an enlightened English teacher foisted *The Pickwick Papers* upon our class when we turned 16. And, of course, when I eventually read what Dickens wrote, I was amazed. After finishing *The Pickwick Papers,* I moved on to *Sketches by Boz, The Old Curiosity Shop* and *A Tale of Two Cities,* with its famous opening lines: "It was the best of times, it was the worst of times, it was the age of wisdom, it was the age of foolishness, it was the epoch of belief, it was the epoch of incredulity, it was the season of Light, it was the season of Darkness, it was the spring of hope, it was the winter of despair, we had everything before us, we had nothing before us, we were all going direct to Heaven, we were all going direct the other way."[1]

What Dickens wrote about the French Revolution perfectly describes the state of Catholic education today: we are living in the best of times and the worst of times too; an age of wisdom and an age of foolishness; an epoch of belief and an epoch of incredulity. It is the best of times because, across the world, parents and teachers are establishing new schools and reforming old ones in line with Catholic teaching. Many of these schools have drawn inspiration from heroic bishops and popes and are staffed by enthusiastically orthodox Catholics. The numbers are encouraging, too. In the USA, almost 2 million students are educated in Catholic schools, while in the UK, a nominally Anglican country, Catholic schools and colleges have a disproportionate influence, educating 800,000 students. The disproportionate influence of Catholic education is even more striking in India, where 8 million students are educated in Catholic schools.

But numbers tell only part of the story, so we could just as easily come to the conclusion that we are living in the worst of times. The religious congregations that played such a vital role in the growth of Catholic education have now all but pulled out of schools in many countries. With vocations drying up and nuns and monks aging, many of the great teaching orders of the 19th and early 20th centuries look like a spent force. Unfortunately, lay Catholics haven't always taken up the slack. Catholic schools often struggle to recruit Catholic headteachers, and practicing

---

[1] Charles Dickens, *A Tale of Two Cities* (Ware: Wordsworth Editions, 1999), 3.

Catholic teachers are like gold dust. Then there's the attrition rate among Catholic children, far too many of whom stop practicing their faith by the time they turn 18. Perhaps that's no surprise when you look at what actually goes on in many Catholic schools. Orthodoxy is sidelined, liberal individualism reigns supreme, and what would have been regarded as foundational knowledge until recently is now a closed book to many students and teachers. A great deal of Catholic education has been secularized, and we are all suffering the consequences.

Pope Benedict XVI and the purpose of education

In other words, the story of Catholic education is complex. The picture contains both darkness and light. Heroism and capitulation stand in close proximity. So let's step back for a moment and think about what we actually want from our Catholic schools and colleges, what the purpose of education really is. When Pope Benedict XVI visited Britain in 2010, he said that "a good school provides a rounded education for the whole person. And a good Catholic school, over and above this, should help all its students to become saints."[2] If that is the purpose of education, then we need to radically rethink what we are doing. What matters is not how many children we educate, the strength of our teaching orders, or the nature of the curriculum. What matters is sanctity. "What God wants most of all for each one of you," Pope Benedict told his audience, "is that you should become holy. He loves you much more than you could ever begin to imagine, and he wants the very best for you. And by far the best thing for you is to grow in holiness." In his typically clear-sighted way, he proceeded to suggest that all the measures by which schools and colleges are usually judged simply don't take us far enough:

> When I invite you to become saints, I am asking you not to be content with second best. I am asking you not to

[2] Benedict XVI, "Address of the Holy Father to Pupils," Vatican website, accessed October 23, 2017. https://w2.vatican.va/content/benedict-xvi/en/speeches/2010/september/documents/hf_ben-xvi_spe_20100917_mondo-educ.html#ADDRESS_OF_THE_HOLY_FATHER_TO_PUPILS.

pursue one limited goal and ignore all the others. Having money makes it possible to be generous and to do good in the world, but on its own, it is not enough to make us happy. Being highly skilled in some activity or profession is good, but it will not satisfy us unless we aim for something greater still. It might make us famous, but it will not make us happy. Happiness is something we all want, but one of the great tragedies in this world is that so many people never find it, because they look for it in the wrong places. The key to it is very simple—true happiness is to be found in God. We need to have the courage to place our deepest hopes in God alone, not in money, in a career, in worldly success, or in our relationships with others, but in God. Only he can satisfy the deepest needs of our hearts.

Pope Benedict's speech should inspire and challenge our Catholic schools and colleges to the core. If the aim of education is to help our children become saints, then all the work on which we set so much store is like a toddler's scribbles in a gallery full of paintings by the Old Masters. So often we are measured by results, which means that we look for results that are measurable, but if the measure of our success is our students' sanctity, then we have a problem. We might look for new markers of success, like the percentage of students still practicing their faith when they leave school or the number of converts among non-Catholic students, but these statistics don't get to the nub of the issue either. Sanctity is an issue for God, not a problem to be addressed by a SMART target.

If helping all students to become saints is our goal—and what a mission statement that is—then our job is to find out what God wants from us and to get on with doing it faithfully. But the tragedy of so many Catholic schools is that they don't have sainthood as their aim. Why not? With centuries of sound Catholic teaching behind them and a wealth of Catholic educational thinking easily at hand, how can so many of our schools and colleges have lost their way so significantly? To answer that question, we need to make sense of the times in which we live.

A secular age

In 2007 Canadian philosopher Charles Taylor published an 896-page book which set out to explain the nature of our secular age.[3] He drew a distinction between the pre-modern era and the world in which we now live by describing the porous self, which was open to God, prayer and the supernatural realm, and the buffered self, which is not. His argument is that belief in God is now "contested; it is an option among many; it is therefore fragile; for some people in some milieus, it is very difficult, even 'weird.'"[4] Taylor's work is too complex to be summarized in just a few sentences, so all I want to do here is pull out a few points that can help us understand the task that confronts us, the task of transforming Catholic education.

The first point is that, in our secular age, Catholic education has to be counter-cultural. Since the default position of our age is secular, even believers can live without taking much notice of anything (or anyone) outside the immanent order. The secular assumptions of our age and the consequent fragility of belief make it unsurprising that schools, even our Catholic schools, are drawn away from orthodoxy as though by a very powerful secular magnet.

Another important insight we can gain from Taylor's work is that the secular assumptions that underpin most students' understanding of the world (and most educational thinking today) go back at least 500 years. We might think that our social, theological and educational problems all arose in the 1960s, but Taylor's work clearly shows that the problems we face today are not unique to the late 20th and early 21st centuries. This means that we should take huge encouragement from educators who have shown us how to succeed in a secularized world—saints like Madeleine Sophie Barat, who founded the Society of the Sacred Heart in the immediate aftermath of the French Revolution, and

---

[3] Charles Taylor, *A Secular Age* (Cambridge, MA: Belknap Press of Harvard University Press, 2007).

[4] Craig J. Calhoun, Mark Juergensmeyer, and Jonathan VanAntwerpen, *Rethinking Secularism* (New York: Oxford University Press, 2011), 49.

John Bosco, who launched his educational revolution in scarcely less propitious circumstances.

A third point to take from Taylor's *A Secular Age* is that a Catholic educational fightback is entirely possible. The dominant secularization narrative of recent years—a narrative drawn from Comte, Marx and Weber—has collapsed under the weight of its own contradictions. God hasn't disappeared. Christianity hasn't faded away. What Taylor calls the subtraction theory has itself been replaced. What was true 2,000 years ago remains true today, which should give us all the encouragement we need to fight the good fight in our schools and homes.

Catholic education can flourish and has flourished in our secular age, but it will only flourish again if we are confident that we are offering our students what they truly need. This may seem obvious, but in a secular age where relativism reigns, many parents and teachers simply don't believe that they have theological truths to pass on. In a recent poll for the Theos think tank, only 31% of parents said that they wanted their children "to hold the same beliefs about whether or not there is a God or Higher Power" when they grow older.[5] More worryingly, the figure for self-defined Christians was only slightly higher at 36%.[6] If we are to transform Catholic education, we need to understand the challenges we face, and one of our main challenges in a secular age is convincing our own people that what we have inherited is worth fighting for.

Tri-band schools

We will look at what this challenge means in practice throughout the book. First and foremost, we need to ensure that the Catholic Faith isn't bolted onto our schools, but instead permeates every aspect of our work. However, as the Bishop of Portsmouth, Philip Egan, pointed out in a recent speech, this is complicated

[5] Olwyn Mark, "Passing on Faith," Theos, accessed October 23, 2017. http://www.theosthinktank.co.uk/publications/2016/10/31/passing-on-faith.

[6] Though that figure can be partly explained by the fact that only 55% of those same self-defined Christians said they believed in God!

now that many of our Catholic schools and colleges are effectively "tri-band," comprising a minority of practicing Catholics, a majority of "not yet practicing Catholics . . . and other Christians," and a third group made up of those of other religions and none, "all of whom desire the values and education the school offers."[7]

If we are to effect radical change in our schools, we need to take this tri-banding seriously. Since we can no longer assume that the Faith will already permeate the curriculum, the ethos, and the teaching staff, we need to find new ways of dealing with the secularizing tendencies in education. How we do this will depend very much on our own particular setting. In some situations it might be possible to set up new schools, where the staff are strongly Catholic; some parents will address the problem by educating their children at home; others will want to intervene boldly in their children's schools. Bishop Egan suggests that the solution lies in clear teaching (for governors, staff and students) and strong leadership, since, without a very clear sense of direction from the top, secular assumptions are likely to seep into everything our schools do. As the second law of thermodynamics doesn't quite say, a secular equilibrium is inevitable in our secular age unless there is a continual infusion of sound Catholic thinking and practice.

Reconnecting education

But we need to do more than provide an infusion of the Faith; we need to do more than simply hold our own. What the gospel requires is that we change the world. So in this book I want to keep the big theological picture clearly in mind while suggesting workable solutions that we can actually implement. I want to

---

[7] "The Future of Our Diocesan Schools," Portsmouth Diocese, accessed October 23, 2017. http://www.portsmouthdiocese.org.uk/bishop/docs/2015 1106-BoP-The-Future-of-our-Diocesan-Schools.pdf. See also "The Future of Our Catholic Schools," Portsmouth Diocese, accessed October 23, 2017. http://www.portsmouthdiocese.org.uk/bishop/pastoral_letters/20161002-Bo P-PL-Catholic-Schools-A4.pdf.

push through the fog of despair that can so easily engulf us and show that change—real change—is possible. By drawing on Catholic teaching and the ideas of a raft of educational thinkers, as well as on my own experiences, I want to share a sense of hope.

In *Beauty for Truth's Sake*, Stratford Caldecott wrote: "The fragmentation of education into disciplines teaches us that the world is made of bits we can use and consume as we choose. This fragmentation is a denial of ultimate meaning. Contemporary education therefore tends to the elimination of meaning—except in the sense of a meaning that we impose by force upon the world."[8] Following where he led, I aim to present a holistic vision of what education can be by looking at a different idea or challenge in each chapter, while always attempting to show how all these solutions and issues are interconnected.

In the first section of the book, I try to lay sound foundations by examining some of the fundamental principles that underlie every aspect of Catholic education, starting with parents as the primary educators, before moving onto the relationship between the past and the present, the place of knowledge and wisdom, the much misunderstood virtue of studiousness, and embodied education.

In the second section, I look more directly at some of the key challenges that Catholic education faces today. Having examined these "counter-positions," as Bishop Egan calls them, I look at some of the problems caused by technology or, more precisely, by what Neil Postman calls Technopoly, the deification of technology and the creation of a culture that "seeks its authorization in technology, finds its satisfactions in technology, and takes its orders from technology" while also promoting the "elevation of information to a metaphysical status."[9]

In the third section I step back from these challenges and focus instead on some of the main drivers of transformation—silence

---

[8] Stratford Caldecott, *Beauty for Truth's Sake: On the Re-enchantment of Education* (Grand Rapids, MI: Brazos Press, 2009), 17.

[9] Neil Postman, *Technopoly: The Surrender of Culture to Technology* (New York: Vintage, 1993), 71.

and slow education—before moving onto the ideas of E. F. Schumacher and others to create some perspective on the work of schools and the work that is done in schools.

But not just in schools. This is a book about education rather than a book about schools because, as Neil Postman once wrote, "It is not written in any holy book . . . that an education must occur in a small room with chairs in it."[10] Catholic education begins with Catholic parents and continues with whomever they entrust their children's care to. Any book about Catholic education must, therefore, cover not just what happens in schools, colleges and universities, but what happens in the home. Catholic education, in other words, is a great deal broader and deeper than we sometimes allow it to be.

There is sometimes a danger that we settle for second best when it comes to the education we give our children, but, as Pope Benedict XVI reminded us, this is not an option if we want them to become saints. The task we face is enormously challenging, but the good news is that, if we are faithful to the commission we have been given and put our trust in God, there is no reason why Catholic education should not be transformed in our lifetime.

[10] Neil Postman, *The End of Education: Redefining the Value of School* (New York: Vintage, 1995), 96.

PART ONE

Foundations

1

Parents
as First Educators

I FIRST DISCOVERED that parents are their children's primary educators when looking for a school for our oldest daughter. A group of parents had set up a Catholic school nearby and were holding an Open Day. As we wandered past colorful wall displays and impossibly small chairs, we met one of these parents, a radiologist, who started to explain their philosophy. It was quite different from anything I had ever heard before. Education, he said, was really the job of parents, and schools were only there to assist; that is what the Church teaches, and so that was what they had put at the heart of their Catholic school's philosophy. Suddenly it all made sense. Rather than have to shoehorn our daughter into an institution that had its own agenda, we were being given the opportunity to entrust her to teachers who would help us do our job.

I was amazed by this simple, but hugely important, piece of Church teaching, yet I shouldn't have been. I was teaching in a Catholic school at the time and had taught in two Catholic schools before that. Having converted from Anglicanism the year before our marriage, I had been a Catholic for a decade. And yet somehow I had missed this teaching. Maybe my own reading hadn't gone deep enough. Maybe the people who ran the schools in which I worked hadn't read deeply enough either. Either way, I, a Catholic teacher and parent, had no idea that the Church teaches that we are our daughter's primary educators—not until a chance conversation with a doctor in a primary school corridor, anyway.

I caught up on my reading after that, starting with the Second

Vatican Council's declaration on Christian education, *Gravissimum Educationis*, which stated that parents "must be recognized as the primary and principal educators" of their children and also that "the family is the first school of the social virtues that every society needs."[1] Referring back to Pius XI's encyclical *Divini Illius Magistri*, it developed these ideas in some interesting ways:

> The family which has the primary duty of imparting education needs the help of the whole community. In addition, therefore, to the rights of parents and others to whom the parents entrust a share in the work of education, certain rights and duties belong indeed to civil society, whose role is to direct what is required for the common temporal good. Its function is to promote the education of youth in many ways, namely: to protect the duties and rights of parents and others who share in education and to give them aid; according to the principle of subsidiarity, when the endeavors of parents and other societies are lacking, to carry out the work of education in accordance with the wishes of the parents; and, moreover, as the common good demands, to build schools and institutions.[2]

This paragraph turns the usual way of understanding education on its head: the role of the state is not to provide education in some sort of paternalistic way, but "to protect the duties and rights of parents" and only "when the endeavors of parents and other societies are lacking, to carry out the work of education" as long as it is "in accordance with the wishes of the parents." When parents insist on a truly Catholic education for their children, they aren't trespassing on the rights of the state. Rather, the state is trespassing on the parents' inalienable rights when it assumes that it knows best. As G. K. Chesterton once wrote, with his usual

---

[1] *Gravissimum Educationis*, 3, Vatican website, accessed October 23, 2017. http://www.vatican.va/archive/hist_councils/ii_vatican_council/documents/vat-ii_decl_19651028_gravissimum-educationis_en.html.

[2] Ibid.

perspicacity: "it is not so much (as poor Conservatives say) that parental authority ought to be preserved, as that it cannot be destroyed."[3]

Home education

It may come as a surprise to parents in the USA, where close to 2 million children are home educated, and even to parents in the UK, where home education is now beginning to become more popular, to discover that home education is illegal in many countries. And yet the Church is quite clear in its teaching. According to the *Catechism*, "The right and the duty of parents to educate their children are primordial and inalienable," and "The state may not legitimately usurp the initiative of spouses, who have the primary responsibility for the procreation and education of their children."[4] Education is our responsibility as parents. It is not a duty we should offload onto others.

This doesn't mean that all Catholics should educate their children at home, but it does mean that our role as primary educators doesn't end the day we wave our children off at the school gates for the first time. If we accept the role of parents as our children's primary educators, it will shape or reshape our whole understanding of education. Neil Postman is surely right to claim "that education is not the same thing as schooling, and that, in fact, not much of our education takes place in school."[5] Education is much more than schooling: it runs deeper and spreads wider than any educational institution can ever offer. We need constantly to return to the essential fact that home sets the standards by which schools, colleges and universities are judged, not the other way round, and that parents are the child's primary

---

[3] G.K. Chesterton, *What's Wrong with the World*, in *The Collected Works of G.K. Chesterton*, vol. IV (San Francisco: Ignatius Press, 1987), 166.

[4] *Catechism of the Catholic Church*, 2221 and 2372, Vatican website, accessed October 23, 2017. http://www.vatican.va/archive/ccc_css/archive/catechism/p3s2c2a6.htm.

[5] Postman, *The End of Education*, ix.

educators not because they start the job that professional teachers finish but because what they say to, or do with, their children is a form of education, for good or for ill.[6]

That is why the *Code of Canon Law* says that "There must be the closest cooperation between parents and the teachers to whom they entrust their children to be educated. In fulfilling their task, teachers are to collaborate closely with the parents and willingly listen to them."[7] We need to collaborate—that is, truly work together—and teachers need not just to listen to parents but to listen *willingly*. Whether we send our children to school or home educate them, we need to remember that we're in charge. On one level, every Catholic parent knows this, and yet, in an age that distrusts authority figures, we can be remarkably quick to trust education "experts" rather than our own well-formed judgments. The weight of societal expectations can very easily influence us into giving the job of education to schools and teachers who may well have quite different values and expectations from our own.

Of course, the reason many parents defer to teachers is simply because they couldn't imagine teaching their children themselves—by which they often mean that they don't believe themselves capable of teaching their children how to read, how to do calculus, or how to get to grips with Physics. Some parents also believe that the relationship they have with their children would be damaged by introducing an element of educational compulsion. Others think their children wouldn't listen to them. What this amounts to is a failure of the parental nerve. The truth is that parents know all they need to know—their children—and everything else can be picked up. If "everything you do with your child is education," then parents are already home educators whether they recognize that fact or not.

---

[6] As Silvana Quattrocchi Montanaro puts it: "everything you do with your child is education." Sofia Cavalletti, Patricia Coulter, Gianna Gobi, and Silvana Q. Montanaro, *The Good Shepherd & The Child: A Joyful Journey* (Chicago, IL: Liturgy Training Publications, 1994), 17.

[7] *Code of Canon Law*, 796, Vatican website, accessed October 23, 2017. http://www.vatican.va/archive/ENG1104/_INDEX.HTM.

Schools and parents

Unfortunately, schools often see parents as the problem—or, if that's putting it too strongly, they are rarely keen to listen willingly to them.[8] Teachers sometimes act as though their job is to keep parents informed about what school is doing for their children, rather than to respond to what parents want for their children. Sending reports home can become a substitute for real engagement, while any parent who challenges the way classes are taught, let alone the content, ends up being regarded as a troublemaker. The flash point is often, but not always, Sex Education. When friends of ours objected to their daughter's class being shown a DVD that was clearly out of line with the Church's teaching, they were told that no one had ever complained before. The parent as primary educator was clearly a concept that had passed that Catholic school by.

In today's society, it is very easy to slip into the parent-as-problem mentality. When giving advice about university applications or careers, it is easy to tell students that it's their choice what they do, not their parents'. However, the Church, as we might expect, gives much wiser advice, denying neither the freedom of the child nor the role of their parents: "When they become adults children have the right and duty to choose their profession and state of life. They should assume their new responsibilities within a trusting relationship with their parents, willingly asking and receiving their advice and counsel. Parents should be careful not to exert pressure on their children either in the choice of a profession or in that of a spouse. This necessary restraint does not prevent them— quite the contrary—from giving their children judicious advice, particularly when they are planning to start a family."[9]

With the full weight of the Church behind us, it shouldn't be

---

[8] According to John Taylor Gatto, "Parents, for the most part, are lied to or told half-truths, as they are usually considered adversaries. At least that's true in every school I have ever worked in." That may be putting it too strongly, but there is some truth in his assessment. John Taylor Gatto, *Dumbing Us Down: The Hidden Curriculum of Compulsory Schooling* (Gabriola Island, BC: New Society Publishers, 2017), 62.

[9] *Catechism of the Catholic Church*, 2230.

beyond our capabilities as Catholic educators to recalibrate our schools to ensure that they are fulfilling their role, carrying out "the work of education in accordance with the wishes of the parents." So how do we begin to effect real change?

Educating the first educators

The first step is to encourage Catholic parents to fulfill their God-given role. As Bishop Egan of Portsmouth recently said, "People often say we are short of priests—we are. Yet the real challenge surely is not a shortage of priests but a shortage of *people*, people truly converted to Christ, who truly love Him and put Him first, who want to take real responsibility for their faith in spreading the Gospel."[10] The tragedy of my friends' Sex Education DVD experience was not simply that their local Catholic school gave them the cold shoulder, but that they were alone in raising concerns. In one of his General Audiences, Pope Francis said, "It is time for fathers and mothers to return from their exile—for they have exiled themselves from their children's upbringing—and to fully resume their educational role. We hope that the Lord gives this grace to parents: to not exile themselves from the education of their children."[11] The key question then is not "What are schools up to?" but "How can we educate the first educators?" To address that problem, we need to take a trip to Washington, DC via the English countryside.

About once a month, a group of parents and teachers meets in rural England to discuss articles from *Humanum Review*, which is produced by the Office of Cultural and Pastoral Formation at the John Paul II Institute in Washington, DC. We see these meetings, not as academic exercises, but as a way of sharing ideas about how to bring up and teach our children. Sometimes we look at book reviews, sometimes at editorials, and sometimes we wander away from the article entirely and discuss the issue at hand,

---

[10] "The Future of Our Diocesan Schools."

[11] Pope Francis, "The Family—15. Education," Vatican website, accessed October 23, 2017. https://w2.vatican.va/content/francesco/en/audiences/2015/documents/papa-francesco_20150520_udienza-generale.html.

whether it be technology in the home, the education of the sexes, or home and neighborhood. I'm not sure we spelt out our thinking before we started, but, if pressed, we would probably say that since children matter, we need to set aside some time to consider how we can best bring them up. Everyone wins when we meet: in a relaxed home environment, the adults enjoy the discussion, each other's company, and the home baking, while the children enjoy playing (and the home baking).

The family is the domestic church, as the Second Vatican Council taught, but that doesn't mean it is complete in itself. It is still part of the wider community and the worldwide church. It needs to give and receive if it is to flourish. Pope Francis is surely right to argue that "a rift has opened up between the family and society, between the family and school, the educational pact today has been broken; and thus, the educational alliance between society and the family is in crisis because mutual trust has been undermined."[12] The daily task of bringing up children can seem a lonely struggle when illness, sleep deprivation or puberty kick in. But we're not meant to go it alone. Families can and should provide mutual support.

We need to find ways to help parents fulfill their God-given role, acknowledging that schools can play their part. Most of the families in our group home educate their children, but there is no reason why similar groups should not be set up by schools. It is vital, though, that these groups should be run by, or at the very least with, parents. Some schools hold talks for parents on a regular basis, but the implicit message is that school knows best: "Here is what you need to do" rather than "What can we learn from each other?" We all need to draw on parents' practical wisdom as well as on teachers' professional expertise.

There are other ways in which schools can reinforce the parents' role. They can teach children about it, for a start. Given how important parents and parenting are, it is remarkable that they are hardly mentioned in schools. Teachers spend a lot of time preparing their students for the future: they help them pass exams; they prep them for college; they give them advice about

---

[12] Ibid.

career choices. And yet the most important job of all—being a parent—is usually passed over in silence. Of course, it is true that children learn about parenting from their parents, but there should surely be at least some room in the curriculum for teaching about child development, parenting and associated topics. Parents should absolutely remain the primary educators in this area, as in all others, but it would be a curious education that failed to back parents up in their role as primary educators.

How else can schools reinforce the parents' role? Parents should be encouraged to be so much part of school life that their presence no longer excites comment. Schools should be places where all generations are welcome. Events should be arranged for grandparents, and no one should be disturbed by the sight or sound of babies and toddlers. The intergenerational strength of the family should spill over into school. Parents should be actively encouraged to serve as school governors—the more of them the merrier. Parents may also be invited to provide in-service training for teachers if they have appropriate expertise. Ways of breaking down barriers between schools and parents should be encouraged if we are to demolish the teacher-knows-best mentality that often reigns supreme.

The spoilt generation

But all these suggestions are predicated on the assumption that parents want to parent. Unfortunately, the evidence is that many parents set limits on their parenting. Walking through a supermarket this week, I saw a mother pushing her baby in a pram. That wasn't remarkable, but the fact that the baby, rather than the mother, was peering intently at a smartphone was. Of course, keeping children occupied isn't straightforward and keeping them quiet is even harder, so it's no surprise that parents look for help wherever they can find it, even if that means turning to Nokia or Apple. If they can't do it on their own, then why not turn to technology for help? Parenting, like all undesirable jobs, has been outsourced.

In *The Spoilt Generation: Why Restoring Authority Will Make Our Children and Society Happier*, Aric Sigman suggests that Britain now has three-parent families, with electronic media as the third parent: "Consider that electronic media now claim more hours, days and years of your child's eye contact and attention than you, their parents, do," he writes. "Baby DVDs, TV, PlayStations, iPod videos, YouTube and social networking are displacing the vital influence of us parents and other key figures in our children's lives . . . often replacing it with something that is very much at odds with effective parenting. And this unrecognized parent in our children's lives is making a decisive contribution to the creation of a spoilt generation."[13]

But technology isn't the only problem. The Theos report I mentioned in the previous chapter paints a worrying picture of parents who no longer parent. The report suggests that "Young people . . . may be less religious than the older generation, not because of a value shift in the importance they place on religion, but on the value and importance that their parents and family have placed on passing it on."[14] In a society that places a high value on tolerance and that has increasingly displaced religion from the public square, it is perhaps no surprise that many parents have a vague sense that they are imposing on their children if they try to pass on their faith: "The value placed on a young person's autonomy is one reason given for failing to prioritize religious transmission," the Theos report says. "This is in line with what is noted to be a distinct feature of religion, indeed of life, in modern Britain, namely a culture shift from obligation to choice. This emphasis on autonomy and choice gives young people, for example, the option of not attending church. Indeed, one might go further than this, to say that attending church is not only one option among many for young people, but is often treated with such derision and disdain in much mainstream culture as to tilt the choice away from serious religious commitment."

We face a situation where parenting is no longer always seen as something parents *do*, but instead as something that happens by default. We may not like consumerism, but we don't want our

---

[13] Aric Sigman, *The Spoilt Generation: Why Restoring Authority Will Make Our Children and Society Happier* (London: Piatkus, 2009), 115.

[14] Mark, "Passing on Faith."

children to feel they're missing out when their peers get the latest gadgets. We may feel uneasy about social media, but we don't believe we can stand out against technological progress. We want our children to practice the faith, but if they want to play hockey, football, or tennis instead of attending Mass, we have to respect their choice. Or so the zeitgeist goes. As a society, we no longer trust parents to bring up their children, let alone educate them, so it's hardly a surprise that so many parents capitulate in front of the secular pressures they face. Nevertheless, there is an alternative. The attitudes revealed in the Theos survey may be dispiriting, but the report itself presents a positive alternative, summarizing research which suggests that:

• Adolescents and young adults who experience or who have experienced close, affirming, and accepting relationships with both parents are more likely to identify with the beliefs and practices of their parents.

• The security and stability of the parent-child relationship, including the strength of the childhood attachment, informs the stability of future religious beliefs.

• The influence of grandparents, and indeed the wider family, plays a positive role in faith formation.

• Authoritative parenting—where the exercise of discipline and control is accompanied by warmth, nurture and responsiveness—is more conducive to religious transmission than authoritarian or permissive parenting.

• The consistency of parental religious practice, which includes the importance that is placed on it and the integrity with which it is exercised—both inside and outside the family home—positively correlates with the practice of adolescents and adult offspring.

• In addition, parental religiosity acts as a stabilizing factor within the family unit, particularly when both parents share and practice the same faith.[15]

[15] Ibid.

In other words, parents really matter, and there's plenty of evidence to prove it. The parent as primary educator is absolutely key to the transformation of Catholic education. In essence, the rest of this book will simply be a deeper exploration of that one fundamental truth. It is because parents matter that schools have a function. They are (or should be), as Jesus Urteaga wrote in *God and Children*, a continuation of home: "any school or college will form its pupils well, according as it resembles a Christian home."[16] So, to finish this chapter, let's look briefly at the role of the teacher and how it ties in with the role of the parent.

The role of the teacher

While there is widespread agreement about the importance of good teachers, there is also widespread disagreement about what that means in practice. Some studies stress the importance of pedagogical knowledge, others of classroom management, and still others emphasize the virtues. But if we look at work that has been done with adopted children and children in care, we can formulate another answer altogether. What makes a good teacher, important studies suggest, are relationships. And not just any relationships, but relationships that develop the parental role.

Attachment theory and recent developments in cognitive science demonstrate that children's early life experiences and, specifically, their attachment to a nurturing adult (usually the parent) have a crucial impact on their ability to regulate emotions and form relationships. However, even without secure early attachments, children are able to move from surviving to thriving by developing those secure attachments after the crucial first years. The teacher is not, therefore, simply someone who teaches. The teacher is someone who is able to act as "a potential *secondary* attachment figure who can help to reshape insecure attachment behaviors and support the development of more secure ones."[17] In other words, whether they know it or not,

---

[16] Jesus Urteaga, *God and Children* (Manila, Philippines: Sinag-Tala, 1984), 97.

[17] "An Introduction to Attachment and the Implications for Learning and Behaviour," Bath Spa University, accessed October 23, 2017. https://www.bath

teachers are helping their students through the relationships they have with them. Through these relationships, teachers are able to develop the primary role of the parents, not by replacing them but by replicating their role in another environment. Whatever a child's family background, teachers are always truly *in loco parentis*. That is what makes their job possible.

So, whether we choose to educate our children at home or at school, we need always to hang on to the fundamental idea that we parents are their primary educators. And if we know this, we need to help other Catholic parents and our Catholic schools discover this liberating truth. The parent is the primary educator, whether we acknowledge it or not. If we are to transform education, we simply need to remember that basic fact and act upon it.

---

spa.ac.uk/media/bathspaacuk/education-/research/digital-literacy/education-resource-introduction-to-attatchment.pdf.

2

The Problem with Presentism

THE IMPORTANCE OF PARENTS as prime educators is clear, but both parents and children have to operate in a culture that sometimes puts obstacles in their paths. Whether we like it or not, we are compelled to work in conditions that are not at all conducive to passing on the faith of our fathers. That is why we need to pay particular attention to a largely unseen obstacle: presentism, which we might define as an excessive interest in the present to the exclusion of the past.

In *From Athens to Auschwitz: The Uses of History*, Christian Meier argues that "we are experiencing more history and historical change than almost any generation before us, and yet we take virtually no interest in it."[1] For Meier, an essential problem of our age is "the absence of history," which, given the plethora of history books, TV documentaries, and historical fiction in contemporary culture, seems surprising. However, what Meier is referring to is not the volume of historical production but rather the absence of "a historical orientation, a historical way of seeing things or asking questions." Speaking in 2010, Pope Benedict XVI said something similar: "Today's culture is in fact permeated by a tension which at times takes the form of a conflict between the present and tradition. The dynamic movement of society gives absolute value to the present, isolating it from the cultural legacy of the past, without attempting to trace a path for the future."[2]

---

[1] Christian Meier, *From Athens to Auschwitz: The Uses of History*, trans. Deborah Lucas Schneider (Cambridge, MA: Harvard University Press, 2005), x.

[2] Benedict XVI, "Meeting with the World of Culture," Vatican website, accessed October 23, 2017. https://w2.vatican.va/content/benedict-xvi/en/

To understand better what Pope Benedict and Christian Meier meant, we could do a lot worse than travel to western Texas, where, deep inside a mountain, a remarkable clock is being built. A clock which only tells the correct time if you ask it. A clock 200 feet tall. A clock whose chimes are designed never to repeat themselves over 10 millennia. It is the 10,000 Year Clock, designed by The Long Now Foundation. I need to issue a word of warning. If you want to see it, you will have to be determined: it is a day's hike from the nearest transport hub. But that's the point. This is a clock that is designed to last, that is meant to remind us of the long-term, that is supposed to force us to think beyond the immediate.

The 10,000 Year Clock is a fascinating response to short-termism, but as Jo Guldi and David Armitage point out in *The History Manifesto*, "Even those who have assigned themselves the task of inspecting the future typically peer only shortsightedly into the past. Stewart Brand's Clock of the Long Now points 10,000 years ahead, but looks barely a century backwards."[3] Trying to escape an obsession with the present, the Long Now Foundation reaches out to the future. What Pope Benedict and Christian Meier suggest is that we also have to reach out to the past.

The problem of presentism

The urgency of this task is suggested by French historian François Hartog who, in two recent books, provides a compelling analysis of what he calls regimes of historicity, society's ways of relating to the past, present and future.[4] For Hartog our current regime of historicity is dominated by "presentism," a sense that "the past

---

speeches / 2010 / may / documents / hf_ben-xvi_spe_20100512_incontro-cultura. html. See also Gilles Lipovetsky, *Hypermodern Times*, trans. Andrew Brown (Cambridge: Polity, 2005), 35–40.

[3] Jo Guldi and David Armitage, *The History Manifesto* (Cambridge: Cambridge University Press), 3.

[4] François Hartog, *Regimes of Historicity: Presentism and Experiences of Time*, trans. Saskia Brown (New York: Columbia University Press, 2015); François Hartog, *Croire en l'histoire* (Paris: Flammarion, 2013).

and the future are represented, thought of, and felt as departing from and returning to the present,"[5] in contrast to previous eras which privileged either the past over the present or the future over both. According to Hartog, the success of the heritage industry, sales of popular history books, and the presence of media-friendly historians on our TV screens cannot hide the fact that, driven by presentist concerns and assumptions, our contemporary culture is largely indifferent to the challenges of the past. In fact, even the terms we use to make sense of the contemporary world are often divorced from history: "this presentist present is surrounded by a series of notions or concepts that are more or less divorced from time: 'modernity' and the 'postmodern,' but also 'globalization' and even 'crisis.'"[6]

Since presentism is what defines our current regime of historicity—a regime shared by students, teachers, and examination boards—it cannot but infiltrate our schools. This is a real problem for a religion that is grounded in history. If God works in history, and if God became man at a particular point in history, presentism should be a real concern for us—especially since presentism exists in, and is a product of, our secular age. As Charles Taylor and José Casanova remind us, "Modern unbelief is not simply a condition of absence of belief, nor merely indifference. It is a historical condition that requires the perfect tense, 'a condition of "having overcome" the irrationality of belief.'"[7]

C.S. Lewis wrote something similar in *The Screwtape Letters*, having the devil Screwtape explain what looks very much like presentism:

[5] Abdelmajid Hannoum, "What is an Order of Time?," *History and Theory* 47 (2008): 458.

[6] François Hartog, *Croire en l'histoire* (Paris: Flammarion, 2013), 290: "ce présent présentiste s'entoure de tout un cortège de notions ou de concepts, plus ou moins détemporalisés: modernité, postmoderne, mais aussi globalisation et meme crise." My translation.

[7] Michael Warner, Jonathan VanAntwerpen, and Craig Calhoun, *Varieties of Secularism in a Secular Age* (Cambridge, MA: Harvard University Press, 2010), 266.

The Historical Point of View, put briefly, means that when a learned man is presented with any statement in an ancient author, the one question he never asks is whether it is true. He asks who influenced the ancient writer, and how far the statement is consistent with what he said in other books, and what phase in the writer's development, or in the general history of thought, it illustrates, and how it affected later writers, and how often it has been misunderstood (specially by the learned man's own colleagues) and what the general course of criticism on it has been for the last ten years, and what is the 'present state of the question'. To regard the ancient writer as a possible source of knowledge—to anticipate that what he said could possibly modify your thoughts or your behavior—this would be rejected as unutterably simple-minded. And since we cannot deceive the whole human race all the time, it is most important thus to cut every generation off from all others; for where learning makes a free commerce between the ages there is always the danger that the characteristic errors of one may be corrected by the characteristic truths of another. But thanks be to our Father and the Historical Point of View, great scholars are now as little nourished by the past as the most ignorant mechanic who holds that "history is bunk..."[8]

But it is not just writers from the distant past who are passed over when presentist assumptions become embedded in our educational institutions and in the wider culture. Louis Dupré reminds us that in "a period of frantic change, no thinkers vanish more rapidly than those of the recent past. Their ideas are not so much refuted as shoved aside for a succession of new ones that address the present more directly. We secretly fear the ideas of the past—not those of the remote past but of the past still remembered.

---

[8] C.S. Lewis, *The Screwtape Letters: Letters from a Senior to a Junior Devil* (London: Macmillan, 1961), 139. See also Lewis's Introduction to *St Athanasius on the Incarnation* (Cambridge: Cambridge University Press, 1989).

Their growing paleness reminds us uncomfortably of the transiency of our own thought."[9]

History and the allure of presentism

So, if, as Pope Benedict XVI, Christian Meier, François Hartog, Charles Taylor, Louis Dupré, and C. S. Lewis argue in their different ways, our secular age is grounded upon a perception of rupture—a sense that past beliefs have to be jettisoned to allow the balloon of the present to fly off into the blue skies of the future—how does this affect Catholic education? Let's start with History, which we might hope would be immune to the allure of presentism. Take this example from a history textbook produced for 11-year-olds, in which students are asked "Why was the Roman army like a top football team?" before being provided with the following activity:

Here are some tips for success in football management.

• Buy the best players from around the world.

• Get them fit! Keep them healthy!

• Pay them well.

• Stay in the best hotels.

• Banish wives and girlfriends (WAGs).

• Clever tactics—use your brain.

• Get your players (and your supporters) to the games on time!

How are these similar to what made the Roman army successful?[10]

Though it could be argued that the approach used here is designed to start with students' experiences and interests in order

---

[9] Introduction to Romano Guardini, *Letters from Lake Como*, trans. Geoffrey W. Bromiley (Grand Rapids, MI: W.B. Eerdmans, 1994), xiii.

[10] Chris Culpin, Dale Danham, Ian Dawson, and Maggie Wilson, *SHP History: Year 7, Pupil's Book* (London: Hodder Education, 2008), 30–31.

to draw them out of the limited sphere of their contemporary experiences and perceptions, it is surely more likely that students are being encouraged to judge the past from the perspective of the present, the Roman army being seen through the prism of contemporary sport.

Abandoning the Middle Ages

A presentist approach to history can also be seen in the Ideas and Beliefs section of the same textbook, with students being asked to consider whether Henry VIII was "medieval or modern." This baffling question is then broken down into the following conundrum: "Were his ideas medieval—just like all the other kings you have studied in this book; or was he a modern man?"[11] In order to answer this question, students not only have to accept that there is a fundamental divide between the "medieval" and the "modern," but they have to ignore the fact that the very word "medieval" sets up a particular way of understanding the relationship between past and present. "Medieval" and "the Middle Ages" are, of course, polemical terms, as Michel Zink has recently argued, building upon what Régine Pernoud and C.S. Lewis demonstrated many years ago.[12] Whether Henry VIII's ideas were "modern" or "medieval" is not, therefore, a neutral question. If "medieval" has connotations of ignorance, a lack of civilization or downright barbarity, then students are being sold a particular view of the past, whatever their judgments on Henry VIII. As Catholic educators, we need to fight these prejudices tooth and nail, and a good place to start would be by abandoning the words "medieval" and "Middle Ages" altogether.

[11] Ibid., 204.
[12] Michel Zink, *Bienvenue au Moyen-Âge* (Paris: Editions des Equateurs / France Inter, 2015); Régine Pernoud, *Pour en finir avec le Moyen Age* (Paris: Éditions du Seuil, 1977), translated as Régine Pernoud, *Those Terrible Middle Ages: Debunking the Myths*, trans. Anne Englund Nash (San Francisco: Ignatius Press, 2000); C.S. Lewis, *Poetry and Prose in the Sixteenth Century* (Oxford: Clarendon Press, 1997).

Middlemarch and Middle Earth

Unfortunately, this presentist contempt for certain aspects of the past can be found not just in history textbooks, but even in the Oxford School Shakespeare edition of *Julius Caesar*, where we are told that, "following Henry VIII's break away from the Church of Rome, all people in England were able to hear the church services *in their own language*. The Book of Common Prayer was used in every church, and an English translation of the Bible was read aloud in public. The Christian religion had never been so well taught before!"[13]

We might write this off as a straightforward example of old-fashioned anti-Catholicism, but what about this? "At the start of the 16th century the English had a very poor opinion of their own language: there was little serious writing in English, and hardly any literature." Hardly any literature? Does the author mean just at the start of the 16th century, or in the thousand years up to that point? *Beowulf, Pearl, The Dream of the Rood, Piers Plowman, Sir Gawain and the Green Knight*, and *The Canterbury Tales* gone in an instant?

In 2013, the British Secretary of State for Education, Michael Gove, gave a speech in which he discussed "the enacted school curriculum"—what is actually taught as opposed to what is available for teaching. Asking his audience to imagine that "you come home to find your 17-year-old daughter engrossed in a book," he posed a straightforward question: "Which would delight you more—if it were *Twilight* or *Middlemarch*?" Later in the speech, he pithily summarized his argument by saying that "Stephanie Meyer cannot hold a flaming pitch torch to George Eliot. There is a Great Tradition of English Literature—a Canon of transcendent works—and *Breaking Dawn* is not part of it."[14] In effect, what Michael Gove was arguing was that presentist attitudes underpin the enacted curriculum. I am obliged by British examination

[13] William Shakespeare and Roma Gill, *Julius Caesar* (Oxford: Oxford University Press, 2001), 121.

[14] "What Does it Mean to Be an Educated Person," Department for Education, accessed October 24, 2017. https://www.gov.uk/government/speeches/what-does-it-mean-to-be-an-educated-person.

boards to teach post-1990 texts, but I am not obliged (or encouraged) to teach anything from the first 800 years of English Literature. The enacted school curriculum has us teaching *Of Mice and Men*, *Animal Farm*, and Carol Ann Duffy's poetry, but the inevitable consequence is that the premodern—the 1000+ years of Catholic literature which could so easily be taught—is not just ignored: it might as well never have existed. For Michael Gove, battle lines are drawn between *Middlemarch* and *Breaking Dawn*. For me they are drawn between *Middlemarch* and *Middle Earth*.

The tyranny of the present

Children rarely learn that our contemporary prejudices might be challenged by the past. As Neil Postman put it with a liberal dose of irony: "Cicero remarked that the purpose of education is to free the student from the tyranny of the present, which cannot be pleasurable for those, like the young, who are struggling hard to do the opposite—that is, accommodate themselves to the present."[15] Whether we like it or not, our children are being sold a grand narrative of History that many Catholic schools are surprisingly reluctant to confront. Cut off from premodern ways of thinking, cut off from ways of thinking that were shaped by our religion, it is no wonder that our children accept secularized notions of what it means to be human. To meet the challenge, we may need to start by changing how we teach History and English, but we will only succeed if we also challenge the presentist assumptions that underpin many other subjects and curricula.

Preparing foundations

In a fascinating essay on "Total Effect and the Eighth Grade," Flannery O'Connor puts forward "the proposition, repugnant to most English teachers, that fiction, if it is going to be taught in the high schools, should be taught as a subject and as a subject with a history" precisely because "many students go to college

---

[15] Neil Postman, *Amusing Ourselves to Death: Public Discourse in the Age of Show Business* (New York: Viking, 1985), 151.

unaware that the world was not made yesterday; their studies began with the present and dipped backward occasionally when it seemed necessary or unavoidable."[16] "Total Effect" is a brilliantly argued (and very funny) essay which argues that our students need to read 18th- and 19th-century fiction before they move on to modern fiction, not simply because modern fiction only makes sense in context but because "in our fractured culture, we cannot agree on morals; we cannot even agree that moral matters should come before literary ones when there is a conflict between them. All this is another reason why the high schools would do well to return to their proper business of preparing foundations."[17]

In *Bienvenue au Moyen Âge*, Michel Zink takes her argument a step further by suggesting that we go back much further than the 18th century. Zink points out that perceptions of the Middle Ages change when we consider them "with the eyes of poetry. Castles and forests, princesses, knights, monsters, marvels and adventures still nourish our imaginations today, for children through the works of Walt Disney and for adolescents through their role-play games, as the imaginations of Tolkien and C. S. Lewis were nourished. The words of the troubadours or of courtly love still make us dream. Neither Roland at Roncevaux nor Tristan and Isolde are forgotten. The Grail never lost its mystery."[18] If we are really going to challenge contemporary prejudices, we need to reach back into pre-modernity.

We have not yet completely lost touch with our Christian heritage, but we do need to re-discover it and find ways of re-present-

---

[16] Flannery O'Connor, *Mystery and Manners: Occasional Prose* (New York: Farrar, Straus & Giroux, 1970), 137–38.

[17] Ibid., 140.

[18] Zink, *Bienvenue au Moyen-Âge*, 13: "Mais tous change quand on regarde le Moyen Âge avec les yeux de la poésie. Châteaux et forêts, princesses, chevaliers, monstres, merveilles et aventures nourissent aujourd'hui encore notre imaginaire, celui des enfants avec Walt Disney, celui des adolescents et de leurs jeux de rôle, comme ils ont nourri celui de Tolkien et de son Hobbit, de C. S. Lewis et du monde de Narnia. Les mots de troubadour ou d'amour courtois font encore rêver. Ni Roland à Roncevaux ni Tristan et Iseut ne sont oubliés. Le Graal n'a rien perdu de son mystère."

ing it, and Michel Zink is surely right that stories are one way in, since pre-modern literature can be an attractive way of challenging presentist assumptions. Pre-modern literature presents readers with stories, characters and symbols that are still deeply attractive, but which exist in a context that is disturbingly unlike our secular age. In reading the stories, admiring the characters and responding to the symbols, we may be jolted out of contemporary assumptions. The function of literature in education, in other words, is not primarily to provide moral exemplars but to shake us out of complacency.

We can also turn to modern authors who have not cut themselves off from their pre-modern Christian forebears. Chesterton, Lewis and Tolkien are rightly lauded in some educational circles (though you would be hard-put to discover them on too many reading lists in the UK), but they are not alone. There are some wonderful contemporary (or near-contemporary) authors whose books can jolt readers out of unthinking presentist assumptions, including Catholics like Tim Gautreaux and George Mackay Brown, Russian Orthodox authors like Eugene Vodolazkin, and even Calvinists like Marilynne Robinson. There is hope in fiction yet.

Music and mathematics

However, it is also true that History and Literature cannot break the stranglehold of presentism on their own. They need support from other disciplines. One of the most powerful of these is music. Listening to BBC Radio 3, the UK's classical music station, I am constantly heartened by references to Catholic beliefs and practices that have all but disappeared from every other area of public discourse. Where else will you hear the *Stabat Mater,* the *Salve Regina,* and the Mass mentioned on a regular basis? Where else will you hear devotions to Our Lady, requiems for the dead, and prayers to God? We sometimes wonder where the next great Catholic novelist or artist is coming from, but there are many highly regarded composers working today—including James MacMillan and Arvo Pärt—for whom Christianity is the central concern. And if we look back through the history of classical music, we find composer after composer who saw no conflict at all between his or her music and his or her vocation: Olivier Messiaen, Sofia Gubaidulina, Alfred Schnittke, Henryk Górecki, François Poulenc, Edward Elgar, Manuel de Falla, Anton Bruckner, Franz Liszt (who received minor orders), Antonio Vivaldi (who was a priest), Hildegard of Bingen (who is a Doctor of the Church). The list goes on and on. That's without even mentioning those minor composers Bach, Haydn, Mozart, and Beethoven. But it's not just the presence of Christians at the heart of the musical world that matters; in this context what matters more is that we clearly cannot write off composers simply because they were working hundreds of years ago. 20th- and 21st-century music can be exhilarating, but no one seriously suggests that we should bin Bach and Beethoven in favor of Boulez and Berio.

The place of Literature, History (including Art History) and Music in any Catholic curriculum might be relatively uncontroversial, but I want to finish the chapter with one subject which is rarely seen as a bulwark against presentism: Mathematics. In *Beauty for Truth's Sake*, Stratford Caldecott reminded his readers that "the four disciplines of the *quadrivium*—arithmetic, music, geometry, and astronomy—had one thing in common: they were based in mathematics."[19] He also suggested that "our present education tends to eliminate the contemplative or qualitative dimension of mathematics altogether, reducing everything to sheer quantity. Mathematics is regarded as a form of logical notation, a mental tool with no relation to truth except the fact that it assists us in manipulating the world."[20] We could go further and say that Mathematics is no longer seen as a subject with a history. It is no longer recognized as a subject that has developed over time and whose foundations were laid down at specific times and in specific places by specific mathematicians. We certainly need to inspire our students with the truth and beauty of Mathematics, but we can also help destroy Screwtape's Historical Point of View by putting Mathematics back in context and history back into

---

[19] Caldecott, *Beauty for Truth's Sake*, 53.
[20] Ibid., 55.

Mathematics. We need to challenge presentism wherever it rears its head, and we must continue doing so until our children are ready to be challenged by the past. That is a foundational task. Only then can we truly begin to teach.

3

Knowledge and Wisdom

ONCE WE HAVE established that parents are the primary educators and that there is more to education than the contemporary, we can move onto the content of the curriculum: what we want our children to learn. Catholic education must always acknowledge that knowledge matters, but such an obvious truism is not always seen to be true. If knowledge matters only when it is seen to be useful or relevant, if skills—especially if they are deemed to be transferable—trump factual knowledge, then much that is genuinely important in education will inevitably be sidelined.

Before we look at what it is that we want our children to learn, therefore, we need to establish (or re-establish) the importance of knowledge itself, and that means refusing to take sides in the sterile debate that pits skills against knowledge. This debate has debilitated educational thinking for too long, but, as a range of recent writers have convincingly shown, the dichotomy between skills and knowledge simply cannot be sustained.[1] Skills cannot be taught in the abstract: they are entirely dependent on knowledge. What's more, they are domain-specific, which means that our children won't become skilled by being taught skills. What they really need is expertise, and to gain expertise they need both knowledge and skills.

---

[1] Daniel T. Willingham, *Why Don't Students Like School?: A Cognitive Scientist Answers Questions About How the Mind Works and What it Means for the Classroom* (San Francisco, CA: Jossey-Bass, 2009); E.D. Hirsch, *Why Knowledge Matters: Rescuing our Children from Failed Educational Theories* (Cambridge, MA: Harvard Education Press, 2016); Daisy Christodoulou, *Seven Myths about Education* (London: Routledge, 2014); Matthew B. Crawford, *The World Beyond Your Head: On Becoming an Individual in an Age of Distraction* (London: Penguin, 2016).

Knowledge remains vital in our technological age, despite repeated claims that the internet has removed the need to actually learn anything. When Helen Czerski, a physicist, oceanographer, and BBC broadcaster, visited the school where I teach, she shocked many in the audience by saying that her students at University College London are not very good at googling. Why not? Because, she said, they don't know enough to be able to google effectively.[2] To use a search engine well, we have to possess a certain level of knowledge. Without it, we flounder in a sea of unprocessed and unprocessable facts (and, since it is the internet we're talking about, in oceans of nonsense too). Knowledge matters, even in the information age; we cannot simply outsource our memories to digital devices.

We are sometimes told that the world is changing so fast that what we teach our students will be out of date before they have time to use it. In the 21st century there is no point using 20th-century tools to cram children full of 19th-century knowledge, or so the slogan goes. If the future is with us already, and if it looks utterly different from what has gone before, then the only educational model that makes sense is that offered by 42, a university with no courses and no professors, a place where "students are actively learning by completing a variety of projects" and where no degrees are awarded because "our program is based on levels of experience that you earn with a project."[3] This is the ultimate in contemporary education: a university that is hierarchically flat, a place where students teach each other. But what is missing from this utopian vision is the crucial insight that knowledge relies on knowledge. Novelty itself relies on old knowledge— contemporary technological advances have not been achieved by abandoning fundamental mathematical or physical rules. The university of the future cannot survive by rejecting everything

---

[2] Of course, she is not the only one to have pointed this out. See also E. D. Hirsch, "You Can Always Look It Up—Or Can You?," accessed October 24, 2017, http://special.edschool.virginia.edu/papers/hirsch_liu.html and Christodoulou, *Seven Myths about Education*, 59–70.

[3] "Disrupting Engineering Education," 42, accessed October 24, 2017. https://www.42.us.org.

that was taught in the past. As Daisy Christodoulou puts it, "Microfiche readers and MiniDisc players have more chance of becoming obsolete than the alphabet or the numerical system."[4] Or, as Ben Goldacre writes, "Archimedes has been right about why things float for a couple of millennia. He also understood why levers work, and Newtonian physics will probably be right about the behavior of snooker balls forever."[5] Science does not progress by rejecting everything that was previously believed: it builds on what went before, even if sometimes bricks need to be rearranged and unsafe structures have to be dismantled. Or, to change the metaphor, it's not just scientists who are dwarves standing on the shoulders of giants. We all are: historians, geographers, linguists, theologians. We cannot simply start afresh. We rely on knowledge that has been slowly accrued.

Knowledge matters

Knowledge matters. Ignorance is not bliss. Rather, it is an open invitation to the worst prejudices of our age. That is why, as Catholic educators, we need to ensure that our students are truly knowledgeable. Covering a colleague's lesson in a Catholic school a few years ago, I was surprised to learn that most of the class (a group of intelligent 16-year-olds) believed that religious belief was entirely a matter of faith—by which they meant that it seemed a nice idea though the facts were against it. "Close your eyes and hope for the best" was what their understanding of faith amounted to. Of course, this is not what faith means, and it is certainly not what the Church teaches. But that was what was holding those students back: ignorance of what the Church actually teaches about faith and reason.

We should never underestimate the difficulties that are caused by straightforward ignorance or simple misunderstanding of what might seem to us basic doctrines and basic vocabulary. If, for instance, students don't know what the Church teaches about

---

[4] Christodoulou, *Seven Myths about Education*, 55.
[5] Ben Goldacre, *Bad Science* (London: Harper Perennial, 2009), 237.

the infallibility of the Pope, then they are bound to have a completely skewed understanding of the Catholic Faith, believing either that the Pope is supposed to be infallible on every question or, since such an idea is obviously preposterous, that he has no magisterial authority at all. (Though "magisterial" is unlikely to be the word they use.) And if they have no idea of what St John Paul II and Pope Benedict XVI, to give just two examples, have written about faith and reason, they will not remain empty vessels waiting to be filled with glorious truth, but instead are liable to swallow vaguely secularist assumptions about the incompatibility of faith and reason, with disastrous consequences for both.

Counter-cultural literacy and unintentional knowledge

Our children need knowledge, but what exactly they need to know is very much an open question, and not just in Catholic schools. The content of the curriculum has been fought over for as long as there have been curricula, though the philosophies underpinning different debating positions have not always been brought out into the open. When E. D. Hirsch published *Cultural Literacy* in 1987, for example, the subtitle he chose was "What Every American Needs to Know." However, as he admits in his most recent book, what he was actually trying to create was "a list of what literate Americans who made a good living and could communicate with other Americans in fact *did* know in 1987, but which less fortunate Americans, who did not make a good living, tended not to know,"[6] adding that a "more accurate subtitle could have been 'What the Middle Classes Know, and You Need to Know to Belong to That Income Level.'" Put like that, the subtitle is not only less catchy, but reveals a set of philosophical assumptions with which Catholics would struggle to concur.

Counter-cultural literacy is what we are after, which means that the content of our curricula cannot simply ape what is found in secular institutions. Furthermore, we need to insist that focus-

---

[6] Hirsch, *Why Knowledge Matters*, 126.

ing on the usefulness of knowledge—what it can do for us—is not the way to create a Catholic curriculum. As Blessed John Henry Newman argued in *The Idea of a University*, knowledge is its own end, which means that "unintentional knowledge" can be as important as "core knowledge."[7] If we concentrate exclusively on whatever is deemed essential by examination boards, school inspectors, or other curriculum planners, there is a real danger that students will shut their minds to anything that is not specifically taught or, even worse, to any knowledge that is not tested.[8] Newman insisted instead that knowledge is "universal," that "all branches of knowledge are connected together, because the subject-matter of knowledge is intimately united in itself, as being the acts and the work of the Creator." As Catholic educators, we need to rediscover the universality of knowledge in an educational world that, to all practical purposes, is designed to compartmentalize it.

What this means in practice will vary enormously from place to place, but often the changes needed will be very simple. Take library design as an example. What do we put on display? Newly-published books? Or old books that might shake us out of complacency with their unfashionable ideas? If presentism is a problem, we need to think carefully about the stock our libraries carry. I sometimes feel that I am on a one-man mission to rescue great books that my local libraries have thrown out. It might be a stretch to suggest that we need to be like 16th-century Catholics

---

[7] Julio Alves, "Unintentional Knowledge: What We Find When We're Not Looking," *The Chronicle of Higher Education*, accessed 24 October 2017, http://www.chronicle.com/article/Unintentional-Knowledge/139891.

[8] Newman writes about "ill-used persons, who are forced to load their minds with a score of subjects against an examination, who have too much on their hands to indulge themselves in thinking or investigation, who devour premiss and conclusion together with indiscriminate greediness, who hold sciences on faith, and commit demonstrations to memory, and who too often, as might be expected, when their period of education is passed, throw up all they have learned in disgust, having gained nothing really by their anxious labours, except perhaps the habit of application." John Henry Newman, *The Idea of a University* (Dublin: Publication of the International Centre for Newman Studies, 2005), 149.

desperately burying their sacred items in the hope that the next monarch might restore the faith, but there is perhaps some merit in ferreting away old books until the happy day when books are no longer discarded simply because they have tatty covers, because they haven't been checked out recently, or because they were published more than ten years ago.[9] Rather than wait until the intellectual climate changes, I have established a library of my own in which discarded books sit alongside new ones. I encourage students to borrow not just university prospectuses and career guides, but books, too, even though (or especially because) they have nothing to do with the official curriculum. This extension library has become a tangible sign of my commitment to Newman's conception of knowledge and liberal education, though I rarely tell my students as much.

A focus on unintentional knowledge does not mean that we should abolish curricula or allow teachers to teach whatever they choose (that would allow the Miss Jean Brodies of this world to rule the roost[10]), but it does mean that we need to give time to truths that are not on the syllabus and which are not going to be tested. Whether we appreciate it or not, we send implicit messages to our students about what really matters through what we do and say. If we only speak to them about exams, then exam results will be all that they are interested in. If, with Newman, we believe in the universality of knowledge, we need to ensure that our structures aren't working against it.

In the school where I work, we tried to break free from this narrow exam-focus by creating a series of staff lectures, freeing our teachers from the restrictions of the curriculum so they could inspire students to enjoy learning for its own sake. The lectures have been more successful than we could ever have hoped: students have turned up in huge numbers; the lectures themselves have been excellent; teachers keep volunteering. What is more, after attending the lectures for a year, some of our older

---

[9] Eamon Duffy, *The Voices of Morebath: Reformation and Rebellion in an English Village* (New Haven: Yale University Press, 2001).

[10] Muriel Spark, *The Prime of Miss Jean Brodie* (London: Macmillan, 1961).

students asked if they could have a go, so we launched a series of student lectures as well. Students have exactly the same brief as their teachers and have risen to the challenge, giving lectures on topics as diverse as the Politics of Remembrance, Bee-Keeping, and the Septuagint.

If Catholic education values the true, the good and the beautiful, we need to look for it—and we need to help our students look, too. The task of Catholic curriculum planners is not to limit the glory of God, but to help children see it, wherever it may be found.

Canonical knowledge

The length and breadth and height and depth of God's wonderful creation should not make us throw up our hands in despair when given the task of choosing what to teach next. We have the Church to guide us. We can rejoice in the liberation that magisterial teaching provides. That is why both unintentional knowledge and what we might call "canonical knowledge" matter.[11] The content of literary and other canons may be a matter of perennial debate in schools and universities, but Catholics have a great advantage in knowing what our canon is. We can, therefore, give our children a thorough education in the doctrines of the faith, confident in what the content of those lessons should be. It might seem obvious that students need to know what the Church teaches, but the case still needs to be made, since there are many who assume that doctrinal truth is simply inaccessible to today's students. That was not Pope Benedict XVI's view when he spoke to Catholic educators in the USA in 2008 or when he spoke to teachers and religious during his visit to the UK.[12] Instead he

---

[11] Canonical knowledge is a term E.D. Hirsch briefly mentions in *Why Knowledge Matters*, though Hirsch and Catholic educators may not always agree about what comprises canonical knowledge.

[12] Benedict XVI, "Meeting with Catholic Educators," Vatican website, accessed October 24, 2017. https://w2.vatican.va/content/benedict-xvi/en/speeches/2008/april/documents/hf_ben-xvi_spe_20080417_cath-univ-washington.html.

spoke about "the self-evident requirement that the content of the teaching should always be in conformity with Church doctrine."[13]

We should never forget that children are more than capable of rising to the challenge of learning the language of the faith, as I was reminded when I introduced my 5-year-old daughter to a spelling game. The idea of the game is for each player to add a letter without completing a word. (The peril of having an English teacher dad is that you have to put up with this sort of thing from a young age.) As my daughter had only just started learning to spell, I had some difficulty getting her to appreciate the nuances of the game. "C," she said. "A," I offered. "T," she shouted triumphantly. Once more I explained that she wasn't supposed to complete the word and we tried again. She started with "D". I added "O". Utterly predictably, she said "G". "OK," I said, deciding to approach the rules from a different angle, "shall we try to come up with a more complicated word this time?" She thought for a moment and then, with a broad smile, announced, "Consubstantial!" Now, I am not claiming that she could spell "consubstantial" (let alone define it) at the age of five, but she certainly knew the word, which is more than can be said for some of my (much older) students.

On another occasion, one of our friends told us about the children's liturgy group she had run that morning. While talking to the children about Heaven, she had mentioned the Second Coming. "Oh, the Parousia, you mean," one of the girls said. She was six years old. Too often we assume that children cannot cope with theological language, but the reality is that they can respond to a great deal more doctrinal knowledge than we often give them credit for. This is not to say that we should be giving five-year-olds a bunch of encyclicals to read, but it does mean that we

---

[13] Benedict XVI, "Address of the Holy Father to Teachers and Religious," Vatican website, accessed October 24, 2017. https://w2.vatican.va/content/benedict-xvi/en/speeches/2010/september/documents/hf_ben-xvi_spe_2010 0917_mondo-educ.html#ADDRESS_OF_THE_HOLY_FATHER_TO_TEAC HERS_AND_RELIGIOUS.

shouldn't hold back when attempting to teach them the essentials of the faith.

Doing so will help us in other educational areas, too. Each year, I have to teach my literature students basic theology before they can make sense of set texts like *The Great Gatsby*. Each year we read sentences like this: "At his lips' touch she blossomed for him like a flower and the incarnation was complete."[14] And each year I have to explain what "incarnation" means. But the problem is not restricted to *The Great Gatsby*: unless students have a reasonable understanding of theological language, they simply cannot access a huge swathe of pre-20th-century literature.

I am not arguing here that every class should become a religion class—Flannery O'Connor rightly reminds us in "The Teaching of Literature" that the teacher's "first obligation is to the truth of the subject he is teaching"[15]—but I am suggesting that if students receive a good scriptural and doctrinal grounding, they will reap the benefits in other subjects. If we ensure that our children know the faith, then most other aspects of their education will also fall into place.

Amusing ourselves to death

Or so we might hope. But if this is the case, why do we have a problem? How can we be in a position where not even Catholic schools can be relied upon to teach Catholic doctrine? One reason is because we have not always paid sufficient attention to the culture in which education happens. In *Amusing Ourselves to Death*, Neil Postman argued that the rise of television had a deleterious impact on every aspect of society, writing that "as the influence of print wanes, the content of politics, religion, education, and anything else that comprises public business must change and be recast in terms that are most suitable to television."[16] This is not the place for an in-depth analysis of Postman's

---

[14] F. Scott Fitzgerald, *The Great Gatsby* (Oxford: OUP, 1998), 89.

[15] O'Connor, *Mystery and Manners*, 128.

[16] Postman, *Amusing Ourselves to Death*, 8. See also Postman, *The End of Education*.

argument, but we should take careful note of his point that it is the *content* of education that must change as the dominant medium of communication changes. *What* we teach changes as well as *how* we teach it. As soon as accessibility trumps analysis, the content of the faith will slowly seep out of our schools.[17]

In our televisual age (and, even more, in our computer age), we have problems convincing pupils, parents and colleagues that there is a problem to be addressed simply because the dominant technologies of our age cut against the acquisition of knowledge, including doctrinal knowledge. The difficulty of our task is compounded by the fact that success clearly *is* possible in our contemporary culture without what we might regard as indispensable knowledge. Listening to a BBC radio program called "A Good Read" recently, I was surprised to hear an award-winning novelist reveal that, until *Northanger Abbey* was chosen for review by her fellow guest, she had never read any of Jane Austen's novels. At school she read "very modern books," but missing out on the classics had not prevented her from developing a career as a successful novelist.[18]

We are bound to come across resistance, silent or otherwise, from those who claim (in some ways quite rightly) that students can survive in the modern world without the sort of knowledge we might think indispensable. We have to face up to the fact that we are going to make ourselves unpopular if we want our children to learn more about the Catholic faith, because there is no easier way of inviting trouble than attempting to change the content of the curriculum in our schools and colleges. But there is no other option. We have to get the basics right. We must lay firm foundations if curricular changes are to make any long-term difference to our children's lives.

---

[17] A point Newman understood: "Recreations are not education; accomplishments are not education. Do not say, the people must be educated, when, after all, you only mean, amused, refreshed, soothed, put into good spirits and good humour, or kept from vicious excesses." Newman, *The Idea of a University*, 144.

[18] For a quite different perspective, see Marilynne Robinson, *When I Was a Child I Read Books* (London: Virago, 2013), 87.

The end of education

However, in the struggle over the curriculum, there is also a danger that we will lose sight of the ultimate end of education. Newman was right to remind us that knowledge is its own end, but it is not the end of education. "Knowledge then," he wrote, "is the indispensable condition of expansion of mind, and the instrument of attaining it; this cannot be denied, it is ever to be insisted on; I begin with it as a first principle; however, the very truth of it carries men too far, and confirms to them the notion that it is the whole of the matter," adding that "the end of a Liberal Education is not mere knowledge." Romano Guardini wrote much the same, arguing that our "educational institutions are means of passing on knowledge. Educated persons are those who have acquired knowledge of all kinds at these institutions. Yet all of this has little to do with true education, since true education is rooted in being, not in knowledge."[19] Speaking in the USA in 2008, Pope Benedict echoed these words: "Truth means more than knowledge: knowing the truth leads us to discover the good. Truth speaks to the individual in his or her entirety, inviting us to respond with our whole being."[20] Or, as he said in the UK: "The task of a teacher is not simply to impart information or to provide training in skills intended to deliver some economic benefit to society; education is not and must never be considered as purely utilitarian. It is about forming the human person, equipping him or her to live life to the full—in short it is about imparting wisdom. And true wisdom is inseparable from knowledge of the Creator, for 'both we and our words are in his hand, as are all understanding and skill in crafts.'"[21] The end of education is not knowledge but wisdom.

Catholic educators will always hold knowledge in high esteem, but if the purpose of education is to help our children become saints, knowledge can never be enough. The Sadducees and Pharisees were knowledgeable, but they did not always possess

---

[19] Guardini, *Letters from Lake Como*, 87–88.
[20] Benedict XVI, "Meeting with Catholic Educators."
[21] Benedict XVI, "Address of the Holy Father to Pupils."

wisdom. Teachers and students may gain an impressive number of qualifications, but there is no certificate for saintliness. If we are to transform Catholic education we need to remember that the end of education is not the accumulation of facts. We need to remember that knowledge needs to lead to wisdom, and that wisdom cannot only (or even primarily) be gained in the classroom.

4

Attention and the
Lost Virtue of Studiousness

IN A RECENT BOOK, the Organisation for Economic Co-opera-
tion and Development (OECD) asks how the learning sciences
can inform the design of 21st-century learning environments and
sets out what it calls seven principles of learning: learners at the
centre; the social nature of learning; emotions are integral to
learning; recognizing individual differences; stretching all students; assessment for learning; and building horizontal connec-
tions.[1] There is a great deal of interest in the book, once we get
past some of the pseudo-business school jargon, but it is not my
intention to scrutinize the OECD's analysis here. What I want to
do instead is to take us back to a profound understanding of
teaching and learning that informed Catholic education long
before we felt the need to replace philosophy with the "learning
sciences." I want to return to St Thomas Aquinas.

Unlike St Augustine, St Thomas Aquinas did not write a trea-
tise about teaching, but he did address the topic in a number of
his books, notably in *De Veritate* and in the *Summa Theologiae*. A
particularly fascinating aspect of St Thomas's account is the way
in which it anticipates the contemporary focus on how students
learn, or, to use the language of the OECD, on how "learners are
the central players in the [learning] environment."

The acquisition of knowledge

According to St Thomas,

---

[1] OECD, *The Nature of Learning: Using Research to Inspire Practice* (Paris:
OECD, 2011).

knowledge is acquired in man, both from an interior principle, as is clear in one who procures knowledge by his own research; and from an exterior principle, as is clear in one who learns (by instruction). For in every man there is a certain principle of knowledge, namely the light of the active intellect, through which certain universal principles of all the sciences are naturally understood as soon as proposed to the intellect. Now when anyone applies these universal principles to certain particular things, the memory or experience of which he acquires through the senses, then by his own research advancing from the known to the unknown, he obtains knowledge of what he knew not before.[2]

There is a great deal that we might want to unpack here, though it is worth noting to begin with that St Thomas's emphasis on the importance of the senses and the significance of the active intellect sound strikingly modern.

St Thomas uses this understanding of how we learn to inform his understanding of the role of the teacher, arguing that the teacher can only succeed in his task if he respects what is already potentially present in the student: "the teacher causes knowledge in the learner, by reducing him from potentiality to act."[3] The image he uses is of the doctor, who "assists nature, which is the principal agent, by strengthening nature and prescribing medicines, which nature uses as instruments for healing." His understanding of the role of the teacher relies, therefore, not just on Aristotle's bold claim at the start of the *Metaphysics* that "All men, by nature, desire to know," and on his argument that "All teaching and all learning proceed from previous knowledge," but also from the notion that the teacher's task is to assist the learner in bringing out what is, at least potentially, already there.

Knowledge "pre-exists in the learner . . . in the active sense," he writes. "Otherwise, man would not be able to acquire knowledge

---

[2] St Thomas Aquinas, *Summa Theologica*, I. 117, accessed October 24, 2017. http://dhspriory.org/thomas/summa/FP/FP117.html#FPQ117OUTP1. See also St Thomas Aquinas, *De Veritate*, 11.

[3] Aquinas, *Summa*, I. 117.

independently. Therefore, as there are two ways of being cured, that is, either through the activity of unaided nature or by nature with the aid of medicine, so also there are two ways of acquiring knowledge. In one way, natural reason by itself reaches knowledge of unknown things, and this way is called discovery; in the other way, when someone else aids the learner's natural reason, and this is called learning by instruction." But learning by instruction is not fundamentally different from learning by discovery, because "the teacher leads the pupil to knowledge of things he does not know in the same way that one directs himself through the process of discovering something he does not know."[4] The implications of this understanding of teaching and learning are highly significant.

St Thomas and contemporary education

Firstly, this understanding strengthens the arguments of those who argue the case for Catholic unschooling, which is not the same as what is sometimes called Radical Unschooling.[5] Catholic unschoolers emphasize learning by discovery without implying that any adult interference in the learning process is detrimental to the child's progress. Secondly, as Jeffrey Bond argues, a truly

[4] See also Aquinas, *Summa*, I. 117: "Now the master leads the disciple from things known to knowledge of the unknown, in a twofold manner. Firstly, by proposing to him certain helps or means of instruction, which his intellect can use for the acquisition of science: for instance, he may put before him certain less universal propositions, of which nevertheless the disciple is able to judge from previous knowledge: or he may propose to him some sensible examples, either by way of likeness or of opposition, or something of the sort, from which the intellect of the learner is led to the knowledge of truth previously unknown. Secondly, by strengthening the intellect of the learner; not, indeed, by some active power as of a higher nature, as explained above, because all human intellects are of one grade in the natural order; but inasmuch as he proposes to the disciple the order of principles to conclusions, by reason of his not having sufficient collating power to be able to draw the conclusions from the principles."
[5] Suzie Andres, *A Little Way of Homeschooling: Thirteen Families Discover Catholic Unschooling* (Lake Ariel, PA: Hillside Education, 2011) and Suzie Andres, *Homeschooling with Gentleness* (Lake Ariel, PA: Hillside Education, 2015).

Catholic understanding of teaching and learning creates a bulwark against postmodern distortions of knowledge and our relation to it: "to learn something in the natural order, we must already know it in some way. Indeed, how can we come to know a thing unless we stand in some prior relation to it? For if we learn something new and objective, we grasp it; but if we grasp it, we grasp it in the recognition that it means something, or is intelligible to the mind, such as it is. That being the case, it follows that we stand in some prior relation to it. This insight is of capital importance, because it suggests that there is a natural order to the mind and thus an order of knowledge that is in accord with reason and nature. It is this that sets the limits to the whole sphere of teaching and learning."[6] This is important because there is a tendency for otherwise informative writers to slip into unwarranted relativism in their attempts to signify the centrality of the student in the teaching and learning process. John Taylor Gatto, for instance, finishes a fascinating passage about teaching and learning by writing that "wherever possible I have broken with teaching tradition and sent kids down their separate paths to their own private truths."[7]

This is not a mistake that Jeffrey Bond makes. He argues instead that "however gifted the teacher, and whatever mode of teaching he employs, the acquisition of knowledge and the inculcation of the intellectual and moral habits necessary to the acquisition of that knowledge are ultimately dependent on the receptivity and will of the student. Nevertheless, the teacher, if he provides a good example, can assist the student even in acquiring these habits. In a very real sense, then, teachers themselves must be students of that which they do not know, not only so that they may continue to learn themselves, but also so that they may provide a living model for their students." The role of the teacher is, in fact, strengthened by a recognition of the primacy of the student in the learning process. Teachers, properly understood, are not there to inculcate but to draw out, and to do so they must be

---

[6] Jeffrey Bond, "The Modes of Teaching," *The Josias*, accessed October 24, 2017, https://thejosias.com/2015/04/16/the-modes-of-teaching-part-iii.

[7] Gatto, *Dumbing Down*, xxi.

the sort of people who recognize that they are also students themselves. Far from diminishing their authority, such a recognition only enhances the trust and respect they gain from their students.

Our schools, colleges and universities could do a lot worse than get to grips with St Thomas's understanding of teaching and learning. We shouldn't need the OECD to tell us that "prior knowledge—on which students vary substantially—is highly influential for how well each individual learns." As in so many of the areas already covered in this book, we already have the resources we need in the Catholic tradition, if only we are prepared to draw on them.

Of course, one reason why schools are unlikely to build in-service training around the work of a 13th-century philosopher is because of the deeply embedded presentism that was the subject of Chapter 2. However, the teachings of St Thomas should give the lie to the widespread myth that, before the enlightened era of compulsory, comprehensive schooling, children were the passive recipients of knowledge forced into them by unsympathetic teachers. It is a myth that is grounded in a broadly presentist set of assumptions and an understanding of educational history that goes no further than the Victorian era, as filtered through one or two dimly-remembered Dickens novels. We miss out on a great deal if we neglect the work of our greatest thinkers. We miss out, for instance, on the virtue of studiousness.

Studiousness

St Thomas was no ivory tower academic: he knew full well that "on the part of his bodily nature, man is inclined to avoid the trouble of seeking knowledge," but he wasn't a cynic either. He also knew that "on the part of the soul, he is inclined to desire knowledge of things."[8] St Thomas taught that we, and our students, are always being pulled in two directions. It is part of human nature to desire knowledge, but it is also part of our fallen

---

[8] Aquinas, *Summa*, II. II., 166.

human nature to avoid the hard work that is needed if we are to gain that knowledge.

We all know about laziness, so I want to concentrate here on our desire for knowledge. This is where St Thomas's teaching can really challenge contemporary educators: "Now just as in respect of his corporeal nature man naturally desires the pleasures of food and sex," he writes, "so, in respect of his soul, he naturally desires to know something . . . [and] the moderation of this desire pertains to the virtue of studiousness."[9]

Studiousness, for St Thomas, is a virtue, but it is very much a lost virtue. It is also widely misunderstood. As Sr Dominic Mary Heath writes in a fascinating article, "For most of us 'studiousness' probably has associations with dusty books, library stacks, and pale-faced scholars who seldom see the light of day"[10]— which is perhaps why some writers prefer to leave the word untranslated, *studiositas* having slightly fewer of the bookish connotations than studiousness. So what did St Thomas mean by studiousness? "Studiousness," he explained, "is a kind of restraint" and, as such, it is an aspect of the virtue of temperance.

The idea that we might need to temper our desire for knowledge—that curiosity (as St Thomas also explains) might be a sin—does not sit well in our contemporary culture and even, I would suggest, in contemporary Catholic educational circles. It is important, therefore, that we look very closely at St Thomas's argument and resist the temptation to reject his ideas as hopelessly outdated.

St Thomas is very clear that "the knowledge of truth, strictly speaking, is good."[11] There is absolutely no sense here that searching for knowledge is wrong or that children should be discouraged from asking questions, or that Catholicism is all about "blind faith" (one of the New Atheists' favorite paper tigers). However, St Thomas also reminds his readers that the knowledge of truth "may be evil accidentally, by reason of some result, either

[9] Aquinas, *Summa*, II. II., 166.

[10] Sr Dominic Mary Heath, "Giving God Our Attention: Learning the Virtue of Studiousness," *Plough Quarterly*, Summer 2017, 38.

[11] Aquinas, *Summa*, II. II., 167.

because one takes pride in knowing the truth, according to 1 Cor. 8:1, 'Knowledge puffeth up,' or because one uses the knowledge of truth in order to sin."[12] Intellectual pride, just as much as other forms of pride, is a temptation to which we are all prone and, just like every other form of pride, it needs to be resisted.

Our desire to study can be inordinate. St Thomas draws on St Jerome's example of priests forsaking the gospels for plays and love songs. Watching plays and reading pastoral idylls are not sinful activities in themselves, but they can become so "when a man is withdrawn by a less profitable study from a study that is an obligation incumbent on him."[13] St Thomas's second example may seem even more remote: he argues that the desire for knowledge can become sinful "when a man studies to learn of one by whom it is unlawful to be taught, as in the case of those who seek to know the future through the demons." This may not be a temptation by which many of us are assailed, but it is a salutary reminder that teachers matter, that there is a great deal more to education than the inculcation of knowledge. If the teacher is morally dissolute he is bound to have a negative and potentially a disastrous impact on his students. St Thomas's third example of how the desire for study can be inordinate is more obviously pertinent to our secular age: "when a man desires to know the truth about creatures, without referring his knowledge to its due end, namely, the knowledge of God."

St Thomas's fourth example is the one that is most likely to baffle 21st-century students and educators. Knowledge of the truth may be evil accidentally, he writes, when a man "studies to know the truth above the capacity of his own intelligence, since by so doing men easily fall into error." St Thomas is not in the business of lowering intellectual bars or dismissing enquiring minds, but he is keen to bring us back to first principles. He reminds us that "man's good consists in the knowledge of truth; yet man's sovereign good consists, not in the knowledge of any truth, but in the perfect knowledge of the sovereign truth, as the

---

[12] Ibid.
[13] Ibid.

Philosopher [i.e., Aristotle] states. Hence there may be sin in the knowledge of certain truths, in so far as the desire of such knowledge is not directed in due manner to the knowledge of the sovereign truth, wherein supreme happiness consists."[14]

Aristotle, as we have seen, believed that all men, by nature, desire to know; St Thomas took this further, explaining that what all men truly desire to know is God. That being the case, anything that distracts us from our true quest is not only sinful, but also necessarily prevents us from acquiring full knowledge and moving toward the supreme happiness that God desires for us. If we do not desire Truth itself, that is to say Truth Himself, then we will never find *eudaimonia*, perfect human flourishing. Sr Dominic Mary is therefore able to explain studiousness "as the virtue that holds the soul's attention to God and to all true things for God's sake," explaining that it is "clearly much more than bookishness. A mind directed to God is a mind disposed for contemplative wonder." What this means is that "it has a particular 'veneration for concrete reality' because it seeks the divine behind everything it sees. Study has value precisely because it leads beyond itself, through contemplation, to God. This is how it makes us happy."[15]

Paying attention to God

Elsewhere she writes that "paying attention to God is perhaps the best definition we can give, not only of the goal of studiousness, but also of that prayer called contemplation."[16] "Attention" is a word that recent commentators have returned to again and again. Stratford Caldecott devoted a section of *Beauty in the Word* to it, arguing, with Simone Weil, that "the real goal of study is the 'development of attention,'" while Matthew Crawford builds a whole book around the importance of attention in an age of dis-

[14] Ibid.
[15] Heath, "Giving God Our Attention," 41. In this passage, Sr Mary Dominic Heath refers to Josef Pieper, *Happiness and Contemplation* (South Bend, IN: St Augustine's Press, 1998).
[16] Ibid., 40.

traction.[17] Writing that "the question of what to attend to is a question of what to value,"[18] he goes on to argue that what distinguishes successful students is "the ability to strategically allocate their attention."[19] This same idea permeates the work of Mihaly Csikszentmihalyi: "How attention is allocated determines the shape and content of one's life"[20] is just one of his many comments on the topic.

It is certainly true that the ability to allocate one's attention wholeheartedly (or even single-mindedly) to the task in hand is a hugely important prerequisite for academic success, but it is not the type of attention that St Thomas and Sr Dominic Mary have in mind. Their understanding of attention differs significantly from the instrumental use of the word because attention, for them, is attention to a person, and, in particular, to God. That is why contemplation, in the words of Sr Dominic Mary, is "a supremely good use of time"[21] and why adoration of the Blessed Sacrament and indeed any liturgical celebration is a great expression of studiousness.

Studiousness and science

Sr Dominic Mary goes on to suggest that talking about contemplative wonder in our secular age is bound to be met with incomprehension: "The problem for most of us is that when we're told 'happiness is contemplation,' what we actually hear is 'happiness is disembodied.' And we simply can't get excited about the prospect of studying for the sake of contemplation because we know, intuitively, that real human happiness never excludes the body."[22] So, one way of developing the virtue of studiousness is to teach

---

[17] Stratford Caldecott, *Beauty in the Word: Rethinking the Foundations of Education* (Tacoma, WA: Angelico Press, 2012), 29–31. Crawford, *The World Outside Your Head*.

[18] Crawford, *The World Outside Your Head*, 5.

[19] Ibid., 16.

[20] Mihaly Csikszentmihalyi, *Flow and the Foundations of Positive Psychology: The Collected Works of Mihaly Csikszentmihalyi* (Berlin: Springer, 2014), 3.

[21] Heath, "Giving God Our Attention," 40.

[22] Ibid., 41.

our children that studiousness is a virtue that can be practiced outside libraries and without books, because our whole body is involved in the acquisition of knowledge: "studiousness begins whenever we begin to observe what *is*."[23] Or, as she explains in more detail:

> We don't have to read textbooks to experience this kind of studious absorption in reality. We can approach nature studiously whenever we see (smell, taste, touch, or hear) biological life unfolding. We can approach human community studiously whenever we observe meaningful patterns in history, politics, literature, or culture. We can approach the mechanical sciences studiously whenever we pay attention to the amazing way things work. And we can approach the Christian faith itself studiously when we immerse ourselves in the sacred words of scripture and the sacred actions of liturgy.[24]

Put like this, we can begin to see how the virtue of studiousness can be applied to quotidian educational practicalities, starting, perhaps counter-intuitively, with science education.

In an essay for *The New Atlantis*, Matthew Crawford criticizes the way science is presented to students as a means to an end rather than as a subject with its own intrinsic pleasures, noting that in "the era of Sputnik, that public good was clear to all: national defense."[25] However, with the Cold War over, scientific education is now promoted as a way of driving economic growth. The problem with this way of promoting science is not just that it's a blunt tool (all STEM subjects are equal, but some are clearly more equal than others) but also that it will fail to convince most sixteen-year-olds, who are likely to be more interested in whether their next lesson is going to be interesting than they are in GDP. A better, and certainly more honest, justification

[23] Ibid.

[24] Ibid., 41–42.

[25] Matthew B. Crawford, "Science Education and Liberal Education," *The New Atlantis*, accessed October 24, 2017, http://www.thenewatlantis.com/publications/science-education-and-liberal-education.

of science education would take as its starting point the realization that the "effort required to learn any subject well can be sustained only if the satisfactions are intrinsic, rooted in the activity of learning itself."[26] The better answer, in other words, would look very much like the one provided 150 years earlier by Blessed John Henry Newman when he argued that knowledge is its own end.[27]

Questions about science education might seem very distant from questions of temperance, but they both stem from the same root question: to what do we pay attention? Since what we pay attention to reveals what we value, questions about temperance must still matter. In an age of distraction, both we and our students can easily be distracted from what truly matters. Distracted by examination results and league tables, by social media and celebrity culture, by whatever our institutions nudge us toward or by whatever is available when we're feeling tired or stressed, we fail to pay attention to the one thing needful. If attention is a finite resource, as Mihaly Csikszentmihalyi insists, we need to take great care that we allocate it where it's really going to make a difference.

---

[26] Ibid.
[27] Newman, *The Idea of a University.*

5

The Body
and
Embodied Education

IN AUGUST 1978, when Karol Wojtyla traveled to Rome to vote for the new Pope, he gave his secretary some time off and took the book he was writing with him, figuring that he could work on it during any downtime between votes. As it turned out, the voting was over in one day. The cardinal electors chose Albino Luciani of Venice, Wojtyla's secretary had to rush back from the beach, and very little, if any, of his book got written.

Returning home, Wojtyla got on with his work. His friends joked with him about how many votes he had received in the papal conclave and life settled back down to normal. However, a mere month after the election of Albino Luciani as Pope John Paul I, some terrible news reached Poland: the new Pope had suffered a massive heart attack and died.

Karol Wojtyla got ready for a return journey to Rome. This time, rather than have another go at writing his book, he took some reading with him. To his fellow cardinals' bemusement, he tucked into a Marxist philosophical journal in the Sistine Chapel while the votes were being counted. As it turned out, knowing what the enemy was thinking came in very useful over the next world-changing decade. But all that was in the future: the immediate task at hand was choosing a new Pope.

This time, the voting took a little longer, and this time Karol Wojtyla didn't return to Poland straight after the election. After two days and eight ballots, the new Pope was chosen: to everyone's surprise, including his own, it was Karol Wojtyla—or, to give him the name he took that day in late September 1978, John Paul II.[1]

The theology of the body

Pope John Paul II has been described by Timothy Garton Ash, Professor of European Studies at Oxford University, as "simply the greatest world leader of our times,"[2] which is quite a claim from someone who describes himself as an agnostic liberal. It would, of course, be a gross exaggeration to claim that it was John Paul II who brought down communism in 1989, but no less a figure than the last Soviet leader, Mikhail Gorbachev, once said that "everything that happened in Eastern Europe would have been impossible without the presence of the Pope." But it's not John Paul II as world leader that I want to write about here. I want to return to that book he failed to write during the papal elections of 1978.

The manuscript may have gone back into a drawer, but it wasn't long before the new Pope dusted it off so that he could start delivering its contents in his General Audiences. These general audiences marked what George Weigel called "a critical moment not only in Catholic theology, but in the history of modern thought."[3] St John Paul II's complex ideas have been described in several different ways (Catecheses on Human Love, an Anthropology of Love, the Theology of the Body) but perhaps the simplest way to describe them is the role of human love in God's plan. In his audiences, he taught that it is precisely in our bodies, with all their imperfections, that God's love is most explicitly revealed. "The body, in fact, and only the body," he said, "is capable of making visible what is invisible: the spiritual and the divine. It has been created to transfer into the visible reality

---

[1] The information in this section is drawn from George Weigel, *Witness to Hope: The Biography of Pope John Paul II* (London: HarperCollins, 2001).

[2] Timothy Garton Ash, *History of the Present: Essays, Sketches, and Dispatches from Europe in the 1900s* (New York: Vintage Books, 2001) 344.

[3] Weigel, *Witness to Hope*, 343.

of the world the mystery hidden from eternity in God, and thus to be a sign of it."[4] This is by any standards a staggering statement—and not just staggering, but wholly counter-cultural. The body isn't an inconvenient embarrassment: it's right at the core of the Faith. It's where we meet God.

As Carl Anderson and José Granados have written, "fallen man regards the body as a jail cell, as a limitation on our freedom and a curtailment of our possibilities. Our own culture typically deals with the body in this way, treating it as if it were some thing outside us, whose existence we accept only to the extent that it provides pleasure, but which we reject as soon as it becomes a source of pain or an obstacle to our desires."[5] St John Paul II challenged this understanding of the body, which can be traced back to Descartes, by returning to God's original plan as set out in the Book of Genesis and, in so doing, turned the Cartesian mistake on its head. Our body is not some thing outside us. We are not ghosts in a machine. As Terry Eagleton put it with a great rhetorical flourish, "We are not present in our bodies in the way that a soldier squats in a tank."[6]

One of the tragedies of our secular age is that this crucial understanding of the body simply isn't recognized by many outside the Catholic Church and even by some within it. Guy Claxton, for example, is as fierce a critic of Cartesian dualism as John Paul II was ("we do not *have* bodies," he writes; "we *are* bodies"[7]), and yet he appears to have no understanding whatsoever of the rich sacramentality of Catholicism. The only mentions Christianity gets in *Intelligence in the Flesh*, his book about embodied psychology, are disparaging comments about St Paul, St Francis and Opus Dei.[8] This is a real shame, not just because of the

---

[4] John Paul II, *Man and Woman He Created Them: A Theology of the Body*, trans. Michael Waldstein (Boston, MA: Pauline Books and Media, 2006), 203.

[5] Carl Anderson and José Granados, *Called to Love: Approaching John Paul II's Theology of the Body* (New York: Random House, 2009), 108.

[6] Terry Eagleton, *Materialism* (New Haven: Yale University Press, 2016), 40.

[7] Guy Claxton, *Intelligence in the Flesh* (London: Yale University Press, 2015), 3.

[8] Ibid., 18–20.

slur against our faith, but also because his own argument about embodied intelligence and the need for an embodied education would be so much stronger if he realized that for many years Catholics have been practicing the type of education for which he calls.

There are many gaps in Claxton's account. He doesn't mention St Thomas Aquinas, for example, who argued that "sensible knowledge" is the "material cause" of intellectual knowledge.[9] (St Thomas was certainly not a Cartesian thinker.) Nor does he refer to Maria Montessori, who once wrote that "in my schools I have taken great care from the very beginning to follow the growth of the child's body."[10] He also fails to mention Sofia Cavalletti, one of Maria Montessori's followers, who created the Catechesis of the Good Shepherd, a remarkable approach to the religious education of children that takes as its starting point a sacramental (i.e., fully embodied) understanding of reality. In a typical atrium (where the Catechesis of the Good Shepherd takes place), you might see children coloring, writing, moving and making, while the catechists quietly assist. In fact, it is this sense of quiet purpose which is most striking about the catechesis. Forget any ideas you might have about children's liturgy sessions: Cavalletti's atria are places of calm focus and attention, built around an embodied approach to catechesis. It is not so much learning by doing as catechesis that refuses to accept any artificial distinction between mind and body. Given these lacunae in Claxton's book, it is hardly surprising that he also misses St John Paul II's Theology of the Body.

However, it is also true that many Catholics have missed it too. What is more, we have to acknowledge that many of our schools, colleges and universities have unwittingly swallowed Cartesian dualism whole, thereby allowing the education they offer to be

---

[9] Aquinas, *Summa*, I. 84: "non potest dici quod sensibilis cognitio sit totalis et perfecta causa intellectualis cognitionis, sed magis quodammodo est materia causae."

[10] Maria Montessori, *The Discovery of the Child* (Delhi: Aaker Books, 2004), 58.

shaped by mistaken notions of the role of the body. So what does an embodied education look like?

Embodied education

Firstly, embodied education sees the relationship between student and teacher as being of absolutely fundamental importance. The teacher is not simply a purveyor of information and the student is not an empty vessel waiting to be filled. What the teacher brings to the classroom and parents bring to the home is all that they are and all that they have experienced. They are people who have lived life, gained knowledge, developed wisdom, loved, suffered, heard good jokes and told bad ones. They are people who have been brought up in one place and traveled to others. They have interests and enthusiasms, skills and expertise. They are not inputters of data.

We could say the same of the students, too. They are people who have lived, loved, suffered, grown and told jokes. (In fact, if my experience as a parent is anything to go by, they probably remember far more jokes than most adults.) Children too have skills, expertise, knowledge and wisdom. They are still growing, they still have much to learn, but they are not passive recipients of whatever we adults choose to feed them. To put it simply, education happens in any encounter between two human beings. Education is all about relationship.

That is why employment practices matter so much. When schools and colleges hire teachers, they need to do a great deal more than simply check academic credentials. Teachers, we are sometimes told, are role models, and this is true, but it is true in a very specific way. They are role models, not in the sense that actors on a distant stage are role models, but in the way that friends and families are. It is the way they interact with other people—what they say and do in and out of the classroom—that has a profound influence on their students. St John Bosco understood this very well, which is why the education he offered his students could never stop at the classroom door.

Of course, no teacher is perfect, but that needn't hold us back, because the teacher's task is to point beyond himself to the source of all truth, goodness and beauty. As the wonderful Franciscan Sisters of the Renewal write in one of their newsletters:

> Every teacher knows that recess is just as important as the lesson planned. Not only do the children need to get their energy out so they can sit still for the Catechism and the Adoration time, but they also need that more relaxed time with us, to know that we are with them. Time spent with the children is time spent communicating to them: "You are worth my time"; "You are valuable to me." It is a ministry of "presence." Our presence prepares them for The Presence Who remains with us always in the Eucharist—even to the end of time.[11]

That is why we need to work with, and support, the teachers we employ to help them be the people their students need, to be people who can be present for their students and so prepare them for the Real Presence. Depending on where we live and work, we may struggle to hire committed Catholics, but that shouldn't stop us from trying to provide children with teachers who teach with their lives as well as their words, nor should it stop us from supporting our teachers wherever they are on their own journey of faith. But we also need to be hard-headed: if there are problems, we need to address them. In particular, we should not be afraid to insist that teachers whose lives are lived in open disregard for the teachings of the Church do not teach our children, because who teachers are, as well as what they know, matters hugely.

The profound importance of the student-teacher relationship should also give us pause for thought when we reach for technological solutions to educational problems. This is perhaps a particular issue for home educators, who may feel isolated or lacking in subject expertise, but it is also a growing issue in schools. How often are we tempted to solve an issue by putting a screen between teacher and student? How often do we act as though education were essentially disembodied?

---

[11] Community of Franciscan Sisters of the Renewal Newsletter, Fall 2017.

Of course, technology needn't necessarily destroy the teacher-student relationship, but we do need to think about the full implications of our choices. Whenever possible, technology should build on an existing relationship and be intended to develop it. One of my former students, for example, developed a great relationship with her singing teacher in the UK. When the student moved to the USA to continue her studies, she persuaded her slightly skeptical teacher that they could continue with their singing lessons by Skype, and indeed the relationship was strong enough to overcome the limitations of the technology. The reason I know this is because I bumped into that same student when she returned to my school during her vacation so that she could have another singing lesson. Back in the UK, she was able to put Skype to one side and work with her singing teacher again in person.

The teacher as craftsman

What this example suggests is that the relationship between teacher and student is essentially the same as the relationship between craftsman and apprentice. The teacher, like the craftsman, is a source of expertise, but that expertise is not merely intellectual. The teacher is also a source of practical wisdom (*phronesis*, to use Aristotle's term) gained through experience. The teacher knows what works and is able to respond to what his students need.

I picked up a flier at an education conference recently that asked me to imagine Colin, an AI Teaching Support. In the world that Colin is supposed to inhabit, "ceiling cameras monitor [the students'] movements and embedded microphones record their conversations," which reminds me, but evidently not the company that produced the flier, of Orwell's 1984. Meanwhile, "behind the scenes, Colin begins to analyse this speech, text, images, and movement to infer the students' understanding and engagement in the collaboration."[12] There are many troubling

---

[12] Pearson, "Find out about the potential for AI in the Classroom and how Colin could work," undated.

aspects to this imagined future, but what is particularly baffling about the whole scenario is that there is no need for Colin. What an AI Teaching Support may or may not be able to do in 2030 is what teachers do already. Real teachers. Real embodied teachers. If teachers are truly present to their students they will pick up the signals (to use an unhelpfully technological metaphor) far better than any artificially intelligent assistant.

If education is to be transformed, we need to put technological temptations to one side and do all we can to develop this understanding of the teacher as craftsman and the student as apprentice. We need to encourage our teachers to develop their academic and practical skills rather than concentrate on helping them gain promotion to roles that remove them from face-to-face encounters with children. We need to provide or support guild-like structures that bring teachers together for mutual support, rather than perpetuate a model that sees the teacher as king of his classroom, subject only to occasional, impersonal inspection, as though he were a boiler that might conk out if not serviced annually. We need to remember that people matter.

The student as apprentice

If the teacher is a craftsman, then we also need to help students become apprentices. How does the apprentice learn? That is a simple question with a complex answer, but we can perhaps boil it down to two essential points. Firstly, the apprentice learns over a long period of time. He needs to spend time with the master craftsman if he is to learn from him. Since a slow burn is absolutely necessary for success, students and teachers who have grown up in an age of instant gratification may well struggle at first, but we need to give both students and teachers the time they really need to learn. Secondly, the apprentice learns by doing—not doing exactly what the craftsman does (it is now clear that students do not learn by pretending to be experts), but doing the tasks that the craftsman chooses for him.[13] What might this mean in practice?

---

[13] Willingham, *Why Don't Students Like School?*, 127–45.

It means that we have to pay much more attention to craft in education. English lessons often focus almost exclusively on literary or linguistic analysis and neglect the craft of writing. It is indeed a craft that can be taught; the beauty of Evelyn Waugh's prose, for example, can be traced back to the care he took over details. Before he became a novelist he considered becoming a cabinet maker, and it shows in his writing. The physicality of writing has its counterparts in other disciplines, too. I recently spent some time in the archives of the School of Oriental and African Studies, University of London, looking at letters sent by Eric Liddell of *Chariots of Fire* fame. Many of these are now available in print, or have at least been summarized in biographies, but actually getting my hands on the originals brought me much closer to the great man. The small, neat handwriting showed me something of his character; the thin writing paper gave me a new insight into the material conditions in which he was working; and the picture of a peony that was painted for him by a grateful Chinese soldier he had saved from the Japanese provided an emotional link that spanned the decades. I spent many years studying History, but almost always at a distance from actual historical documents. We are not always doing our students a favor when we give them snippets of information in glossy modern textbooks.

Learning through the soles of our feet

The physicality of education should be even more apparent in other subject areas. Geography as we now understand it is a subject built on the understanding that we learn "through the soles of our feet."[14] Fieldwork is absolutely essential. It is only when we get out and about that we can truly understand the land. Science too depends on experimentation. Experiments are the very

---

[14] Simon Springer, "Learning Through the Soles of Our Feet: Unschooling, Anarchism, and the Geography of Childhood," in *The Radicalization of Pedagogy*, eds. Simon Springer, Marcelo Lopes de Souza, and Richard J. White (London: Rowman & Littlefield, 2016), 247–65.

basis of empiricism, yet in class, frequently because of concerns about health and safety, we often do the experiments for our students. Allowing our children to experiment for themselves, to get their hands dirty, is essential. As I type this, an image of my great-uncle flashes into my head. When I was young I was fascinated by his little finger: it was only half there because he had blown off the other half while experimenting with some noxious mix of chemicals.[15] I shall not be repeating his approach! We need to be responsible, but if our default position is that we can read about experiments in books or, worse still, look them up on the internet, we will have neglected some of the greatest pleasures and learning opportunities available to us as educators.

Home educators often speak about the delight that children have in being outside. Certainly our own experience of home education is that our daughter has spent more time outside (in the garden, at the local stables and elsewhere) than she ever did when she was at school, even though sport was a regular feature on the timetable and gardening club was one of the extra-curricular options. This enthusiasm for learning outside should not be thought of as wishy-washy Romanticism. As Josef Pieper reminds us, we have largely lost the crucial sense that the understanding is both *ratio* and *intellectus*:

> *Ratio* is the power of discursive, logical thought, of searching and of examination, of abstraction, of definition and drawing conclusions. *Intellectus*, on the other hand, is the name for the understanding in so far as it is the capacity of *simplex intuitus*, of that simple vision to which truth offers itself like a landscape to the eye. The faculty of mind, man's knowledge, is both these things in one, according to Antiquity and the Middle Ages, simultaneously *ratio* and *intellectus*; and the process of knowing is the action of the two together. The mode of discursive thought is accompanied and impregnated by

---

[15] See Oliver Sacks, *Uncle Tungsten: Memories of a Chemical Boyhood* (London: Picador, 2016) to get a flavor of the era in which Sacks and my great-uncle grew up.

an effortless awareness, the contemplative vision of the *intellectus*, which is not active but passive, or rather receptive, the activity of the soul in which it conceives that which it sees.[16]

Too often we focus on *ratio* to the detriment of *intellectus*. We prioritize discursive, logical thought and ignore the power of sheer receptivity. G.K. Chesterton knew better when he wrote that "the world will never starve for want of wonders; but only for want of wonder."[17] If Pieper and Chesterton are right, then the recent flurry of interest in outdoor education makes perfect sense: it is a genuine response to a genuine loss.[18]

This desire for an education that takes note of our embodied natures has often been expressed in the Forest School movement, which is itself a response to the Scandinavian concept of *friluftsliv*. Forest Schools promote "regular opportunities to achieve and develop confidence and self-esteem through hands-on learning experiences in a woodland or natural environment with trees."[19] I will write more about this sort of education in Chapter 10 but for now I want simply to suggest that observing the passing of the seasons, growing vegetables, and looking after animals are not idle pastimes that give us time out from real work. If St John Paul II is right about what it means to be human, then our education has to be embodied. It should not be resolutely desk-based.

It is very easy to use misleading metaphors in the field of education, but the "field of education" is not one of them. Biological metaphors are much more helpful than technological ones. David Gelernter has recently written about the tides of mind,

[16] Josef Pieper, *Leisure, the Basis of Culture* (San Francisco: Ignatius Press, 2009), 28.

[17] G.K. Chesterton, "Tremendous Trifles," Project Gutenberg, accessed October 24, 2017. http://www.gutenberg.org/files/8092/8092-h/8092-h.htm.

[18] See, for example, Helen Macdonald, *H is for Hawk* (London: Vintage Classic, 2016), Richard Louv, *Last Child in the Woods* (North Carolina: Algonquin Books of Chapel Hill, 2006), and anything by Robert Macfarlane for evidence of this ongoing interest.

[19] "What is Forest School?," Forest School Association, accessed October 24, 2017, http://www.forestschoolassociation.org/what-is-forest-school.

arguing that the brain is fundamentally unlike a computer.[20] Theodore Roszak argued much the same in the 1980s, suggesting that "in little things and big, the mind works more by way of gestalts than by algorithmic procedures."[21] If the mind does not proceed by way of algorithms and if it has tides that ebb and flow, there are some crucial implications for the way we educate. Gelernter suggests that "most people's mental energy or focus level seems to rise as they gradually come awake until a mid-morning maximum; then, focus declines until midafternoon. After this midafternoon drowsiness point, energy and focus level drift back up again until early or midevening, when the downward stretch begins."[22] Most schools do not respect this pattern, and it might be argued that there is no way they could possibly do so, simply because "people's inner clocks differ greatly" which means that no "workday schedule could possibly be ideal for more than a small fraction of workers."

Even so, we have to ask whether it should be our structures that drive the education we give our children, or our children who create the structures. Clearly home educators have a great advantage here; they can be far more flexible with their timetables if they choose to do so. Many home educators begin by mimicking the routines and approach of school in their own homes, but loosen up over time. Some of them feel guilty about this, feeling that they are not doing a proper job, but in fact what they are doing is responding to the people their children are. We were not designed for 9 to 5 and we certainly weren't designed to move from one set of desks to another every time a bell rings, like Pavlovian dogs removed from their natural environment. If the brain is not a computer, we shouldn't expect students to act like machines or keyboard operators. Because they are people and not machines, they live and grow: their embodied nature needs to be respected.

---

[20] David Gelernter, *The Tides of Mind: Uncovering the Spectrum of Consciousness* (New York: W.W. Norton, 2016).

[21] Theodore Roszak, *The Cult of Information: The Folklore of Computers and the True Art of Thinking* (London: Paladin, 1988), 242.

[22] Gelernter, *The Tides of Mind*, 61.

The pedagogy of place

If education needs to be embodied then we also have to think about what David Orr, Professor of Environmental Studies at Oberlin College, has called the *pedagogy of place*. He argues convincingly that "the design of buildings and landscape is thought to have little or nothing to do with the process of learning or the quality of scholarship that occurs in a particular place. But, in fact, buildings and landscape reflect a hidden curriculum that powerfully influences the learning process. The curriculum embedded in any building instructs as fully and as powerfully as any course taught in it. Most of my classes, for example, were once taught in a building that I think Descartes would have been proud of."[23]

Orr explains in great detail what buildings teach, but what it often boils down to is that "the lesson learned is mindlessness, which is to say, [a typical educational building] teaches that disconnectedness is normal," which brings us back to Stratford Caldecott's *cri de coeur* about the fragmentation of education that I mentioned at the start of the book. Teachers certainly think about the rooms in which they teach. They think carefully about how best to arrange desks, and they may well spend a long time on wall displays. But educators rarely go any further. The fact that we speak about classroom management tells its own tale. Neither classes nor classrooms (nor time, for that matter) need to be *managed*. What we need instead is to consider the lessons that our teaching spaces give.

Again, home educators have an inbuilt advantage. What home teaches is that our lives are not fragmented. We need food and sleep and leisure and work. We need to be inside and out; we need sound and silence. No one would think about lining up serried rows of desks in their own home. There is no need for parents to have an electronic whiteboard before they can communicate with their children. Home educators do not need

---

[23] David Orr, *The Nature of Design* (New York: Oxford University Press, 2002), 128. See also David Orr, *Hope is an Imperative* (Washington, DC: Island Press, 2011).

to create a separate schoolroom, as though schools provided the ideal. Instead, teaching and learning in the home is the model to which schools and colleges should aspire.

Thinking about the pedagogy of place brings us finally to liturgical reform. We don't usually associate liturgical reform with the design of school buildings, but the two issues are inextricably linked. This is not the place for a full exploration of the liturgical changes that have taken place since Vatican II, so I will limit myself to observing that the battle over such issues as active participation, the place of the altar, and whether Mass should be celebrated *ad orientem* is so heated partly because all sides agree that what churches look like and how they are arranged really matter. And these issues matter for our students too. If we are to transform Catholic education, we cannot neglect the liturgy. Providing regular access to Mass, Adoration and Confession is really important, but it is not simply the number of opportunities students have to access the rites and sacraments of the church that matters. We also need to ensure that what our students learn from school chapels matches the doctrinal teaching we provide in the classroom. If our chapels are brash or ugly or neglected, our children will pick up implicit messages about the Faith and our attitude toward the Faith. If our liturgies are casual or noisy or rushed, they will similarly receive a lesson we haven't set out consciously to teach. If the sacraments matter, then education must be embodied. And if education is embodied there is no better place to start than with Mass.

PART TWO

Challenges

6

Science and Scientism

HAVING LOOKED AT some of the foundations of Catholic education, it is time to address some of the key challenges, which means being clear about what the key challenges are. So let's get one point straight at the start of this chapter: there is no quarrel between the Church and science. In fact, if Peter Hodgson (who was head of the Nuclear Physics Theoretical Group at Oxford University) is right, science as we know it today only became a possibility in the Judaeo-Christian world. According to Hodgson, "The essential presuppositions of science, that matter is good, orderly, rational, contingent and open to the human mind, are all to be found in the Old Testament. In the absence of these beliefs modern science never developed in primitive societies or in any of the ancient civilizations."[1]

Why was it, Hodgson asks, that despite the otherwise formidable achievements of the Ancient Greeks, the Aztecs, and the Chinese, science in its fullest sense didn't develop in those societies? One reason he gives is that, for science to work, it has to be believed that the universe operates according to consistent patterns or rules and that these rules are discoverable by the human mind, both of which make sense within a Christian framework of ideas. Science also depends upon the idea that the universe is contingent, that it could have been different, which is why scientists have to carry out experiments. The Greeks were great philosophers, but they were not scientists because they didn't appreciate this simple fact. The contingency of the universe is a

---

[1] Peter E. Hodgson, *Theology and Modern Physics* (Aldershot: Ashgate, 2005), 224.

fundamental Catholic belief: not only did the universe have a beginning, but God could have made it differently.

Belief in a contingent universe is crucial, but it is not the only reason why science developed in Christian Europe rather than in Ancient Greece or China. As Hodgson explains,

> The birth of Christ further ennobled matter and replaced the debilitating cyclic time of previous civilizations by a linear time of purpose and progress. . . . The birth of modern science finally took place in Europe in the High Middle Ages when for the first time in history there was a civilization permeated by Christian beliefs. . . . This is not to say that modern science could never have developed in the absence of Christian revelation, but in actual historical fact it did not. Science does not easily take root in non-Christian countries and it languishes wherever Christianity is persecuted or ignored. The historical connection between modern science and Christian revelation does not, by itself, prove the truth of Christianity but, at the very least, it shows that they are in essential harmony.[2]

In books like *Science and Providence: God's Interaction with the World*, John Polkinghorne, who was Professor of Mathematical Physics at Cambridge University before he became an Anglican priest, went even further. He argued that modern science actually makes belief in the Christian God more rather than less possible. When the Newtonian model of the universe ruled supreme—when God was regarded as little more than a blind watchmaker who wound up the universe and then stood back to watch it tick—the Christian God who got involved, who loved and answered prayers, didn't seem credible. But in a universe in which quantum mechanics has extended Newtonian Physics, the Christian God makes perfect sense, as do prayers and sacraments.[3]

---

[2] Ibid., 224–25.

[3] John Polkinghorne, *Science and Providence: God's Interaction with the World* (Cambridge: International Society for Science and Religion, 2007).

There is no conflict between the Catholic worldview and the scientific worldview, and yet the dominant ideology of our age is that Christianity in general, and Catholicism in particular, has a problem with science. One of our tasks as Catholic educators is to bust this myth. We can be proud of the fact that the founder of the modern science of genetics, Gregor Mendel, was an Augustinian monk, and that the Big Bang theory was first proposed by an astronomer who also happened to be a priest, Georges Lemaître.

The challenge of scientism

There is no quarrel between the Church and science, but we are fundamentally opposed to scientism, which, as St John Paul II explained in *Fides et Ratio,* is "the philosophical notion which refuses to admit the validity of forms of knowledge other than those of the positive sciences." The problem with scientism (as opposed to science) is that it sets itself up as an alternative religion, relegating "religious, theological, ethical and aesthetic knowledge to the realm of mere fantasy."[4]

Of course, Catholics are not alone in spotting that scientism works to debase both knowledge and science. Neil Postman has a wonderful chapter on the topic in *Technopoly* in which he argues that three inter-related ideas create the problem of scientism:

> The first and indispensable idea is . . . that the methods of the natural sciences can be applied to the study of human behavior. . . . The second idea is . . . that social science generates specific principles which could be used to organize society on a rational and humane basis. This implies that technical means—mostly 'invisible technologies' supervised by experts—can be designed to control human behavior and set it on the proper course. The third idea is that faith in science can serve as a compre-

[4] John Paul II, *Fides et Ratio*, 88, Vatican website, accessed October 24, 2017. http://w2.vatican.va/content/john-paul-ii/en/encyclicals/documents/hf_j p-ii_enc_14091998_fides-et-ratio.pdf.

hensive belief system that gives meaning to life, as well as a sense of well-being, morality, and even immortality.[5]

The first and third of Postman's points are very similar to St John Paul II's, and the second is strikingly similar to something Pope Francis wrote in *Laudato Si'*:

> It can be said that many problems of today's world stem from the tendency, at times unconscious, to make the method and aims of science and technology an episte- mological paradigm which shapes the lives of individuals and the workings of society. The effects of imposing this model on reality as a whole, human and social, are seen in the deterioration of the environment, but this is just one sign of a reductionism which affects every aspect of human and social life. We have to accept that technologi- cal products are not neutral, for they create a framework which ends up conditioning lifestyles and shaping social possibilities along the lines dictated by the interests of certain powerful groups. Decisions which may seem purely instrumental are in reality decisions about the kind of society we want to build.[6]

The statistical fallacy

But the particular issue from Postman's chapter that I want to pick up on here is his demolition of the idea that "without num- bers [we] cannot acquire or express authentic knowledge" and, particularly, his reminder that "assigning marks or grades to the answers students give on examinations" is a relatively new approach that was introduced by an obscure Cambridge aca- demic in 1792. We may take it for granted that students' work has to be graded, but Postman is surely right when he argues that to say that "this man's essay on the rise of capitalism is an A- and

[5] Postman, *Technopoly*, 147.

[6] Pope Francis, *Laudato Si'*, 107, Vatican website, accessed October 24, 2017. http://w2.vatican.va/content/francesco/en/encyclicals/documents/papa-fr ancesco_20150524_enciclica-laudato-si.html.

that man's is a C+ would have sounded like gibberish to Galileo or Shakespeare or Thomas Jefferson." He is also right to point out that the "idea that a quantitative value should be assigned to human thoughts was a major step toward constructing a mathematical concept of reality."[7]

I have lost count of the number of meetings I have sat through in which teachers discussed possible changes to the school's grading system. These meetings are always unsatisfactory and inconclusive because they are based on a fundamental category error. Children are not computers. They cannot be broken down into their constituent, binary parts. They are human, and so they grow. By all means stand them against a door and measure how much they've grown in the last six months, but let's not kid ourselves that there is any meaningful equivalent of a height chart for knowledge and wisdom. "What can be explained statistically is complicated personally," as Daniel Pennac puts it in *School Blues*.[8]

So why do we continue to treat children as though they were computers? Because many schools, like many businesses, are now dominated by the need to justify their work, which now means providing quantitative markers of success, even though what truly matters in education is, by definition, unmeasurable. The statistical imperative has become so deeply embedded in the way schools work that we no longer notice its presence or its negative effects. And it is scientism that generates, or exacerbates, this belief that everything which is of value must be measured or must, at the very least, be measurable.

One reason the statistical imperative is so problematic is because, inevitably, teachers start to shape their teaching around what can be quantified. Tests proliferate and students focus on learning only what they know will be tested, which wouldn't be so bad if it weren't for the difference between long-term and short-term memory. However, the sad truth is that children are very good at learning what they need to get them through the

---

[7] Postman, *Technopoly*, 12–13.

[8] Daniel Pennac, *School Blues* (London: MacLehose Press, 2010), 1.

next academic hoop and are perfectly capable of forgetting what they have just learned if they do not consider it significant enough to commit to their long-term memory. Learning is therefore very patchy: the irony of the statistical fallacy is that it actually makes education less rigorous.

We also have to acknowledge that schools are very partial about what they measure. They are not so interested in collateral damage—in quantifying the number of students who are put off Math or Physics or French for life. They are not so interested in measuring how much students retain once they have left school. And, though they may pay lip service to their students' long-term progress, they do not focus on the kind of people their students will eventually become, because it is not something they can measure. It is not a metric they are ever going to be judged against.

A further problem was suggested by John Holt, who argued that when "we constantly ask children questions to find out whether they know something (or prove to ourselves that they don't), we almost always cut short the slow process by which, testing their hunches against experience, they turn them into secure knowledge. Asking children questions is like sitting in a chair which has only just been glued. The structure collapses."[9] As I shall argue in Chapter 10, students' learning takes time, so any attempt to measure work and progress is bound to be partial at best and misleading or damaging at worst. Such an approach might sound hopelessly idealistic and impractical, but it works perfectly well for countless home educators. Schools are often built around testing regimes and so school leaders find it hard to imagine how education could be otherwise. What generations of home educators have shown is that testing can either be minimized or dispensed with altogether.[10]

---

[9] John Holt, *How Children Learn* (London: Penguin, 1991), 141.

[10] Gina Riley & Peter Gray, "Grown Unschoolers' Experiences with Higher Education and Employment: Report II on a Survey of 75 Unschooled Adults," *Other Education: The Journal of Educational Alternatives* Vol. 4, Issue 2 (2015): 33–53.

Fides et Ratio

In *Fides et Ratio*, St John Paul II developed his critique of scientism by arguing that it "dismisses values as mere products of the emotions and rejects the notion of being in order to clear the way for pure and simple facticity. Science would thus be poised to dominate all aspects of human life through technological progress. The undeniable triumphs of scientific research and contemporary technology have helped to propagate a scientistic outlook, which now seems boundless, given its inroads into different cultures and the radical changes it has brought."

He further argued that

> regrettably, it must be noted, scientism consigns all that
> has to do with the question of the meaning of life to the
> realm of the irrational or imaginary. No less disappointing
> is the way in which it approaches the other great
> problems of philosophy which, if they are not ignored,
> are subjected to analyses based on superficial analogies,
> lacking all rational foundation. This leads to the impoverishment of human thought, which no longer addresses
> the ultimate problems which the human being, as the
> *animal rationale*, has pondered constantly from the
> beginning of time. And since it leaves no space for the
> critique offered by ethical judgment, the scientistic mentality has succeeded in leading many to think that if
> something is technically possible it is therefore morally
> admissible.[11]

In a society that values freedom—defined in a particularly debased way—above all else, it is no surprise that what is technically possible quickly becomes what is morally admissible, which often enough then becomes morally essential. Our struggle against the horrors of abortion and euthanasia is, more often than not, frustrated by the fact that we are no longer in a position where we can debate the morality of the issues. Euthanasia may

---

[11] John Paul II, *Fides et Ratio*, 88.

still be illegal in the UK, but every time a British citizen flies to Switzerland for a lethal injection, there are calls for a change in the law to meet the "new reality." The ethics of the issue are bypassed altogether. Much the same is true of abortion. If abortion pills are available online, then, the argument goes, we should provide abortion more readily on the NHS rather than allow women to risk their lives on pills whose provenance they cannot know. Arguments like these lead to a fundamental dehumanization of society and a weakening of our life-affirming Catholic anthropology. As Pope Benedict argued in *Caritas in Veritate*: "The supremacy of technology tends to prevent people from recognizing anything that cannot be explained in terms of matter alone."[12] He also wrote that:

> One aspect of the contemporary technological mindset is the tendency to consider the problems and emotions of the interior life from a purely psychological point of view, even to the point of neurological reductionism. In this way man's interiority is emptied of its meaning and gradually our awareness of the human soul's ontological depths, as probed by the saints, is lost. *The question of development is closely bound up with our understanding of the human soul*, insofar as we often reduce the self to the psyche and confuse the soul's health with emotional well-being. These oversimplifications stem from a profound failure to understand the spiritual life, and they obscure the fact that the development of individuals and peoples depends partly on the resolution of problems of a spiritual nature.[13]

One of the difficulties with scientism—and not just scientism but consumerism and relativism too—is that it is largely implicit. It is now so much part of the baggage our students carry with

[12] Benedict XVI, *Caritas in Veritate*, 77. Vatican website, accessed October 24, 2017. http://w2.vatican.va/content/benedict-xvi/en/encyclicals/docume nts/hf_ben-xvi_enc_20090629_caritas-in-veritate.html.

[13] Ibid., 76.

them that they scarcely notice the burden. That is why, to change the metaphor, we need to nail it whenever we can.

Practical measures

What does this mean in practice? As Catholic educators, we should fight tooth and nail against the drive to measure students and schools. We should treat people in a truly humane way, valuing them for who they are rather than for their output. We should also educate parents, teachers and students about Catholic Social Teaching, which provides a comprehensive, attractive and realistic vision of society to set against the limited vision offered by scientism and scientistic ideologies of the left and right. Furthermore, when theological and philosophical knowledge is regarded as unscientific and therefore invalid, we should insist on the place of philosophy and theology in our schools.

Through philosophy and theology we can begin to unpick some of the damage done by scientism by dealing with its effects: when values are dismissed as mere products of the emotions, we can challenge the woolly thinking; when the question of the meaning of life is consigned to the realm of the irrational or imaginary, we can argue the contrary position; and when discussions of the soul's health are reduced to questions about emotional well-being, we can call on the wisdom of those saints whose profound teaching has gradually disappeared from view.[14]

But we also need to address scientism whenever and wherever it appears, which means that teachers and parents need to be philosophically and theologically well-informed. They need to have the wherewithal to defend the faith. That doesn't mean that they all need a degree in Theology and Philosophy, but it does mean that they need to be "prepared to make a defense to any one who calls you to account for the hope that is in you."[15]

Since scientistic problems can appear both in and out of lessons, we need to remain vigilant. We should look at what goes on in science lessons, but we should also pay close attention to

[14] See Ibid.
[15] 1 Peter 3:15.

assemblies, for example, where questions of value and meaning are par for the course, and to school debates, where those same questions are interrogated.

Assemblies are also often woeful in Catholic schools (and elsewhere). If a school has lost its Catholic *raison d'être* then assemblies and other whole school events are usually the first to suffer the consequences. They can become vague to the point of insipidity but, worse still, they can become a bare field on which any philosophy can be played out. Or rather, they become palimpsests, on which some of the values of earlier generations can still be seen, though overwritten by all sorts of post-Christian philosophies. Assemblies can easily become free-for-alls, zones where any passing philosophy can make an appearance. It should not be controversial to argue that assemblies and other whole school events in Catholic schools should be free from ideologies that are antithetical to the Faith.

Debates present a slightly different challenge. Clearly they need to be occasions when differences of opinion are expressed, but there is a danger that, in practice, they simply reinforce the prejudices of our age. Why should this be the case when they appear to offer an ideal opportunity to skewer twisted thinking? The first reason is because the parameters of any debate are set by the motion, and it is entirely possible to have debate after debate that simply accepts the premises of secular liberalism. The second reason is that there is no reason why students' scientistic thinking should ever be challenged if the role of the teacher is limited to chairing or judging the debate. Too often student debates are built upon an inadequate educational philosophy, one which insists not on the importance of truth and knowledge but on challenge and novelty.

By suggesting that scientistic thinking can appear in assemblies and debates, I am not arguing that science lessons are immune from the same problems—we should absolutely insist that what is taught in science labs is in line with Church teaching—but there is no reason to believe that scientism will appear in science more than in other lessons. We should also remember that a balanced curriculum provides a powerful counter-balance to scientism, which is one reason why the Liberal Arts model is so much stronger than the single-subject model found in most British universities. Students are much less likely to be conned into thinking that religious, theological, ethical and aesthetic knowledge are pure fantasy if they are studying a broad curriculum. If they study Theology, the Arts, Humanities, and Science, they are less likely to be seduced by scientism's jealous claims, since scientism, black-hole-like, sucks all other forms of knowledge into itself.

Lake District studies

Another way of countering scientism is to draw our students' attention to the many scientists who are also Christian believers. One of my more unusual qualifications—OK, definitely my most unusual qualification—is a Postgraduate Diploma in Lake District Studies. I was fortunate enough to be taught by some wonderful teachers, including John Rodwell, who, as well as being Professor of Plant Biology at Lancaster University and a globally acknowledged authority on British plant communities, is also an Anglican priest.

I shouldn't have been wholly surprised. When I was an undergraduate, the chaplain of my college was Dr David Atkinson, who later became an Anglican bishop and whose PhD was in Chemistry. The more I looked, the more I noticed people who crossed the alleged science-religion divide: Fr Stephen Dingley, who has a PhD in Radio Astronomy from Cambridge University and a degree in Fundamental Theology from the Pontifical Gregorian University; Fr Andrew Pinsent, who has PhDs in both Particle Physics and Philosophy and who, before he became a priest, worked at CERN, Geneva; the list goes on.

It is not difficult for Catholics to see why some scientists should reject Christianity, but it is much trickier for the New Atheists (who are particularly strident in this area) to explain away the continuing presence of Christians working in the sciences. If Christianity is no more than a crutch, then why should intelligent scientists like Francis Collins and Russell Stannard (to name a couple more) fall for it?

The presence of believing scientists is a powerful witness, but it is not enough in itself to convince skeptical teenagers that scientism should be swept away. To do that we also need to dismantle the entrenched historical myth of conflict between science and religion.[16] Then we need to return to science itself.

Like a mind directed to God, science also has a veneration for concrete reality. Its weakness is its tendency to drift into scientism, but its strengths are real. One of the reasons we should embrace scientific study is because, in an age that is increasingly fixated on visual representations, science brings us back to hard facts.[17] Empiricism is important. Experiments are good for children. Getting our hands dirty is fundamentally good. If we can skewer the false ideology of scientism, we can restore science to its proper place of honor in the Catholic curriculum.

[16] Stephen M. Barr, *Science and Religion: The Myth of Conflict* (London: Catholic Truth Society, 2011).

[17] See Fabrice Hadjadj, "Rediscovering the 'Language of Wood': Why Can't We Just Substitute 'Be Fruitful and Multiply' with 'Connect and Download'?," *Humanum Review* 2015, Issue 4, accessed October 24, 2017, http://humanumreview.com/articles/rediscovering-the-language-of-wood-why-cant-we-just-substitute-be-fruitful-and-multiply-with-connect-and-download.

7

Anthropological Confusion, Consumerism, and Relativism

SCIENTISM MAY BE a jealous god, but it exists in a polytheistic universe; it is not the only idol, or even necessarily the most powerful idol, our children might be tempted to worship. The main problems students face in science, and indeed in many other, lessons are often not scientistic but anthropological. When they are taught about artificial birth control or in-vitro fertilization, they are in danger of being sold an inadequate understanding of what it is to be human. These lessons do not usually proceed from the belief that non-scientific forms of knowledge are invalid, but from secularized understandings of the human person, since we can no longer assume that our relational nature and the intrinsic dignity of the person are notions that will be accepted by either students or teachers in the early 21st century.

What it means to be human

What it means to be human, what it means to be man or woman, and how we should live in a society that challenges our fundamental beliefs about humanity are the key questions of our time. Benedict XVI pointed out that "in order to educate, it is necessary to know the nature of the human person, to know who he or she is. The increasing prominence of a relativistic understanding of that nature presents serious problems for education, especially moral education, jeopardizing its universal extension."[1] In similar vein, G.K. Chesterton once claimed that "we do not disagree, like

[1] Benedict XVI, *Caritas in Veritate*, 61.

doctors, about the precise nature of the illness, while agreeing about the nature of health."[2] What he wrote then is even more obviously true today: we no longer agree about what health is; we no longer agree on what it is to be human.

If we are to transform Catholic education we need to recognize that the challenge of scientism quickly merges into the problem of anthropological confusion, which requires its own response. As a first step, we need to help our children recognize that what it means to be human is a question that needs to be answered, rather than a set of facts that has already been established by the forces of secular modernity. The speed with which topics such as gay marriage and transgender rights have appeared on the political agenda may have surprised us, but we need to face the unpleasant reality that there is already a generation of students for whom secular assumptions on these issues are the norm. The power of presentism, to pick up on the theme of Chapter 2, is such that even recent changes to the ethical and political environment can appear old hat to our children.

And it's not just our children who need to be challenged by the radical truths of orthodox Catholicism in the face of these newly dominant secular orthodoxies. The power of secular assumptions lies in their ubiquity. They are so widely accepted, so widely promulgated, and so actively reinforced that we can all unwittingly be influenced by them. If our students are to discover that the glory of God is a man fully alive, then we need to work with parents as well as with children. If we are to ensure that an adequate anthropology permeates every part of the curriculum, we need to teach the teachers too, recognizing that much of the teaching even in Catholic schools and colleges is widely off-beam because teachers, even Catholic teachers, can unwittingly or uncritically accept secular conceptions of human nature.

And what is the dominant conception? According to Sr Dominic Mary Heath, it is this: "Secular modernity has its own beliefs about the order inherent in the very nature of things, and the first of these assumptions is that there are no spiritual natures in things. Its view of the human person is essentially materialistic

---

[2] Chesterton, *What's Wrong With the World*, 41.

and, consequently, individualistic. That's why its moral code can so seamlessly unite relativism to utilitarianism: Do what you want! But be useful!"

What Sr Dominic Mary calls "deep-set cultural imperatives" have a fundamental impact on our approach to education. "A materialistic, therapeutic culture like this," she writes,

> can give only two reasons for study. Study is either a way for each of us to express our own distinctive personality or a way for us to produce something useful for the world. Ideally, it's both. This explains, for example, why higher education today has become an increasingly bizarre mash-up of obscure fields of study on the one hand and highly technical, professional degrees on the other. Cafeteria-style education—seemingly all-pervasive—makes perfect sense if the order inherent in the very nature of things is actually a dictatorship of our material and psychological urges. Studiousness in this context is a "virtue" only in the sense that it is a habit we need to achieve our cultural goals of originality and self-sufficiency. Studiousness, understood as a virtue directing us toward a moral goal we call "the Good," is essentially lost.[3]

Anthropological confusion

This anthropological confusion can throw all our work into disarray. Some of our students may have difficulty believing in God, or accepting what the Church teaches about God, simply because they have a warped understanding of what it is to be human. If, for example, they have internalized the arguments of radical feminism, they are going to struggle to accept God as a loving father, the male priesthood and the importance of Christian service. But it works the other way round too. If students have only a limited understanding of God, they will also find it difficult to get to grips

---

[3] Heath, "Giving God Our Attention," 40.

with what it is to be human. As the fathers of the Second Vatican Council put it in one of the most profound passages of *Gaudium et Spes*: "Christ, the final Adam, by the revelation of the mystery of the Father and His love, fully reveals man to man himself and makes his supreme calling clear."[4] It is Christ who fully reveals man to man himself. Having fallen from original perfection, we cannot work out what it is to be fully human on our own.

But if we are to remedy such anthropological confusion, we need to accept that much of our work will have to be indirect. We don't need to work on humanity to develop fully human students. Rather, we need to focus on God. Developing, or bringing back, a rich liturgical life is vital if we are to help our students discover what it is to be human. If Christ "fully reveals man to himself," there can be no false dichotomy between worshipping God and learning more about our humanity. The truth is that if we become more faithful Christians then our schools will become more essentially Catholic, and if our schools become more essentially Catholic then our students will become more vitally human.

Hyperconsumption

But a false anthropology is not the only issue holding our children back from being fully human. They face other pressures, including consumerism and relativism. In *The Shift: The Future of Work is Already Here*, Lynda Gratton, Professor of Management Practice at the London Business School, makes a curious claim: "The Industrial Revolution," she writes, "brought a mass market for goods, and with it a rewiring of the human brain towards an increasing desire for consumption, and the acquisition of wealth and property."[5] In this bleak analysis of human nature, consumerism is no longer a choice or a temptation but an essential aspect of our lives. Gratton doesn't dwell on her point about the

---

[4] *Gaudium et Spes*, 22, Vatican website, accessed October 24, 2017. http://www.vatican.va/archive/hist_councils/ii_vatican_council/documents/vat-ii_cons_19651207_gaudium-et-spes_en.html.

[5] Lynda Gratton, *The Shift: The Future of Work is Already Here* (London: William Collins, 2014), 12.

"rewiring" of the human brain because her point seems so obvious: consumption has become such an integral aspect of life in the western world that any further discussion seems superfluous. We may question Gratton's understanding of neurology, but it is certainly true that consumerism is a huge issue for parents and teachers who hope to educate children about the true, the beautiful and the good. So, before we get to grips with how educators can respond to the consumerist environment in which we now operate, we need to examine the nature of that environment.

According to French political philosopher Gilles Lipovetsky, we don't yet live in the postmodern world of which other philosophers have written:

> Far from modernity having passed away, what we are seeing is its consummation, which takes the concrete form of a globalized liberalism, the quasi-general commercialization of lifestyles, the exploitation 'to death' of instrumental reason, and rapid individualism. . . . The State is on the retreat, religion and the family are being privatized, a market society is imposing itself: the cult of economic and democratic competition, technocratic ambition, and the rights of the individual all go unchallenged.[6]

There is a great deal we could pick up on here, but I want to restrict myself for the moment to Lipovetsky's perception that what all this leads to is what he calls a "mania for consumption" or "hyperconsumption." What characterizes our contemporary era, he argues, is that we have moved from "a capitalism of production to an economy of consumption."

Lipovetsky's work is very far from being a rant against the shallowness of contemporary life. He is much more interested in demonstrating how consumerism has changed over time and in charting its impact on people and society. In doing so, he creates a persuasively subtle account of the challenges we have as Catholic educators. In his analysis, hyperconsumption is not simply a "fever for immediate satisfactions" because "the aspirations

---

[6] Lipovetsky, *Hypermodern Times*, 31.

towards a playful and hedonistic lifestyle" are "enveloped in a halo of fears and anxieties."[7] In fact, what characterizes our present age, he thinks, is a "paradoxical combination of frivolity and anxiety, euphoria and vulnerability, playfulness and dread."[8] This is a great description of many students today and, it hardly need be said, a state of affairs that is not at all conducive to deep learning.

What we may well see in our students is, on the one hand, a tendency to trivialize the sacred, the profound or the important, and, on the other, a deep anxiety about the future. That is one reason why they turn so easily to consumerist pleasures: "Through 'things,' what is being expressed, in the final analysis, is a new relationship to personal existence, just as if people were afraid of getting bogged down, of not being ceaselessly provided with new sensations."[9] But we should not be lulled into thinking that consumerism has simply become a quest for personal meaning: according to Lipovetsky, it has a societal, even global, reach: "What characterizes hyperconsumption or globalized consumption is the fact that even the non-economic sphere (family, religion, trades unionism, education, procreation, ethics) is invaded by the mentality of consumer man."[10] Every aspect of our lives, and the lives of our students, is touched (in the western world at least) by the hand of hyperconsumption. That is why it presents one of the most powerful challenges to true Catholic education.

When hyperconsumption invades every sphere of life, it becomes invisible. When it infiltrates family, religion, trades unionism, education, procreation, and ethics, it becomes so close that we fail to notice it. Consumerism is not a cuckoo that pushes chicks out of the nest but a parasite that eats them up from inside. It is only when the empty shell remains that we realize that the life blood has been long sucked out. Consumerism, in other words, is not an aspect of modern life that can co-exist with

[7] Ibid., 45–46.

[8] Ibid., 40.

[9] Ibid., 83–84.

[10] Ibid., 84. In this context see John Taylor Gatto's argument about the difference between a network and a community in Gatto, *Dumbing Down*, 45–69.

a God-oriented existence. It reshapes the religious and educational landscapes as surely as it shapes every other aspect of contemporary society.

However, paradoxically, the very pervasiveness of consumerism provides us with an opportunity to kick back against it. Students raised in an age of environmental concerns and ethical investments may well respond to Pope Benedict XVI's analysis of the *effects* of consumerism and his invitation to "contemporary society to a serious review of its life-style, which, in many parts of the world, is prone to hedonism and consumerism, regardless of their harmful consequences. What is needed is an effective shift in mentality which can lead to the adoption of *new life-styles* 'in which the quest for truth, beauty, goodness and communion with others for the sake of common growth are the factors which determine consumer choices, savings and investments.'"[11] Truth, beauty and goodness remain attractive. The shallowness of consumerism will never be enough to satisfy human needs.

Relativism's sleeping gas

What students are much less likely to recognize is the power of relativism, to which consumerism is closely related. According to Matthew Crawford, the consumer self is a product of "the market ideal of choice" and an "attendant preoccupation with freedom."[12] If I am used to having freedom in every area of my life and believe that I have the moral right to freedom (conceived as

---

[11] *Caritas in Veritate*, 51. See also Lipovetsky's warning: "These days, young people start to become anxious about their choice of studies and the job those studies might lead to at a very early age. The Damocles sword of unemployment is impelling students to opt for prolonged courses of study, and to engage in a race for qualifications that are considered an insurance for the future. Parents too have taken on board the threats linked to hypermodern deregulation. [...] It is training for the future that comes first; hence the vice, in particular, of educational consumerism, private lessons, and non-basic activities outside school. Their aim is to prepare young people for adult life but also, at the other end, to find long-term financial solutions for their retirement." Lipovetsky, *Hypermodern Times*, 46.

[12] Crawford, *The World Beyond Your Head*, 93.

the right to do whatever I like), then I am likely to behave as though no creed or moral code has any more validity than any other. That is why consumerism is so closely related to relativism.

Relativism is like sleeping gas. It permeates the atmosphere and dulls us to the point of immobility, which makes it very hard to deal with. However, though we may not be able to deal with the gas of relativism at source, we can pump fresh air into the room to dissipate its worst effects. The most effective response to relativism and consumerism is authentic Catholicism. If we can introduce our students to truth, goodness and beauty, there will be no need for them to be dulled by the shallow energy-sapping gas of relativism. And, if relativism is, at least in part, a product of one very limited understanding of freedom, we can encourage our students to think about what it means to be really free.[13] If we can show our students that they are most free when they are as they were designed to be, not when they do whatever they like, we will be well on our way toward removing the scourge of relativism from our schools.

---

[13] Edmund Waldstein, "Contrasting Concepts of Freedom," *The Josias*, accessed October 26, 2017. https://thejosias.com/2016/11/11/contrasting-concepts-of-freedom.

8

The Secularization of Happiness

ALL PARENTS WANT their children to be happy, so we might want to celebrate the fact that happiness is big news in the world of education. When, in 2006, Anthony Seldon, Master of Wellington College, announced that he was introducing "happiness and positive psychology" lessons to the curriculum, he was widely ridiculed. But now, ten years later, his ideas have become mainstream. Happiness lessons, wellbeing classes, mindfulness sessions: all these are now staple fare in our schools. But what does this mean in practice and do they work?

To answer those questions, we need to look beyond the world of education because it is not just schools that are focusing on happiness. In 2010 the British Prime Minister, David Cameron, announced a plan to measure national wellbeing, prompting headlines like "David Cameron aims to make happiness the new GDP" and "David Cameron: I want to make people feel better." Nor was he the only politician to pick up on the idea. There has also been a return of happiness in Chinese socialist discourse, with the Communist party under Xi Jinping drawing on the ideas of economist Hu Angang, who proposed a Gross National Happiness Index to help promote progress in his country. From Conservatives to Communists, happiness is the order of the day.

When Anthony Seldon launched his educational reforms, he explained that "Helping to produce happy young adults when they leave the school at 18 is my highest priority as head. I have been saying this for 10 years, but only in the past year have I begun to realize this isn't just an airy-fairy aspiration, but one can in fact learn happiness in classes." What this meant in practice was that:

Pupils will learn about how to form healthy and sustaining relationships. They will gain understanding about the goals they should want to set in life, which should be realistic and appropriate for their own talents and interests. The negative emotions which are an inevitable part of life will be explored: pupils will be able to learn more about what it is that causes them pain and unhappiness, how they might be able to avoid or minimise these emotions and how to deal with them when they do occur. So the essence is that pupils learn more about themselves, which will be information which they will be able to use for the rest of their lives.[1]

In other words, Seldon's lessons were as much about "wellbeing" as they were about "happiness" and, despite the rather hippie terminology, there was much in these lessons that we might approve of. Seldon argued that the lessons would be "highly moral," that "good relationships, which lie at the heart of anyone's happy life, are based on a strong moral code of caring for the other and being loyal," and that "the pursuit of true happiness is also a deeply spiritual quest." Seldon is certainly not a card-carrying Catholic (his explanation of "the heart of spirituality" is that it is "about the transcendence of one's own self and the forming of deeply loving and compassionate relationships with others" rather than a relationship with God), but his approach was clearly one that could be adapted by Catholic schools.

Varieties of happiness

The problem was that the vagueness of the terminology used by proponents of happiness lessons meant that dangerously individualistic and relativistic ideas could infiltrate otherwise helpful lessons. We only have to look at Paul Dolan's *Happiness by Design: Finding Pleasure and Purpose in Everyday Life* to see what could

---

[1] Anthony Seldon, "Lessons in Life: Why I'm Teaching Happiness," *The Independent*, accessed October 24, 2017. http://www.independent.co.uk/news /education/education-news/lessons-in-life-why-im-teaching-happiness-61033 54.html.

appear under the multi-colored happiness umbrella. Dolan's book contains statements that are almost guaranteed to tip you off your chair in disbelief: he argued, for instance, that "the effects of DVDs and KFCs need to be assessed according to their consequences for happiness, and not on the basis of any other judgments, moral or otherwise, about the 'goodness' of these activities."[2] It doesn't seem to matter what the film is actually about, how it makes you behave, or its long-term impact as long as it makes you feel happy. In another part of the book, he wrote, "The good news is that divorce, in Britain at least, has been shown to improve the happiness of the divorcees and their adult children (aged eighteen to thirty) after the knot is broken"[3]— which, as far as he was concerned, seemed to settle the issue. Maybe these quotations, ripped from their original context, look worse than they really are, but even with that caveat, Catholic educators would want to riposte that happiness is not the greatest virtue and that the goodness of a DVD or a marriage cannot be limited to the capacity of either to create happiness, temporary or otherwise. To put it simply, unless happiness education is placed on a firm Christian foundation it can very quickly become all about me, me, me.

The issue is well expressed by Mike Lambert, Headmaster of Dubai College, who has pointed out that, just as there are two quite different approaches to Christmas, so too there are two fundamentally different approaches to happiness education:

> The first argues that happiness results from the pursuit of personal pleasure and the reduction of personal pain. This definition of happiness is ultimately bound up in our narcissistic and materialistic age of consumerism, in which self-satisfaction is seen as the ultimate prize. Advocates of this type of happiness are the Christmas shoppers as it were.

> ...

[2] Paul Dolan, *Happiness by Design: Finding Pleasure and Purpose in Everyday Life* (London: Penguin, 2015), 19.
[3] Ibid., 17–18.

A second school of thought, however, argues that a life lived in consideration of others is the only way to achieve true happiness, since happiness is actually a collective rather than an individual outcome. These are the people who traditionally campaign for shelter for the homeless during the biting winter months and work in soup kitchens on Christmas Eve. For these people, their privileged Christmas meal only tastes good if they know they have done something to help their fellow man.[4]

Lambert argues that it is entirely possible to have "a double helix of happiness lessons, those that enable personal joy and but also those that engender a sense of collective social responsibility in our future generations." It is certainly true that "personal joy" need not be bound up with narcissism and that children with low self-esteem may well need to learn to be happy. Even so, there is a natural suspicion among Catholic educators about the very concept of happiness lessons because of their association with some of the most superficial aspects of our age.

Eudaimonia

However, there is more to happiness than contemporary superficiality. Rather than give up on the whole notion of wellbeing, some Catholic educators have opted instead for classes that take their inspiration from Ancient Greek notions of *eudaimonia*, which is usually translated as "human flourishing." Greek notions of human flourishing seem to foreshadow Jesus's words to his disciples: "I came that they may have life, and have it abundantly." Aristotle's sense that true human flourishing is achieved through the practice of specific virtues has been particularly inspiring.

Catholics are not alone in turning to the virtues. The University of Birmingham, for example, has set up a centre for character and virtues while, even more remarkably, the University of Leeds

---

[4] Michael Lambert, "Should We Be Teaching Children About Happiness in Schools?," *The National*, accessed October 24, 2017. http://www.thenational.ae/opinion/should-we-be-teaching-children-about-happiness-in-schools.

now offers school students a Narnian Virtues Programme. Not so very long ago this would have seemed desperately old-fashioned (and maybe it still does to many) but, with the backing of respected academic institutions behind them, so-called Narnian virtues (which are, of course, solidly Christian virtues) are now able to effect positive change. Education in the virtues ought to be rich territory for Catholics and we desperately need to recover Catholic teaching in this area if we are to transform education.

True happiness, practical happiness

But before we go any further we need to be clear about what we mean by happiness, which takes us back to Pope Benedict XVI's salutary reminder that "true happiness is to be found in God."[5] Without this fundamental realization, any happiness education is doomed to failure. We may find temporary happiness in KFCs or DVDs, but we will never find lasting happiness. As St Augustine told us long ago, our hearts are restless until they find their rest in God.

As Catholics, we can have confidence in what we have to offer. We don't need the exquisitely-named Journal of Happiness Studies to remind us about "Failure-Related Action Orientation and Life Satisfaction: The Mediating Role of Forgivingness"[6] because we already know about forgiveness. And we don't need what Arianna Huffington in *Thrive* calls "the latest scientific findings" to tell us that "if we worship money, we'll never feel truly abundant. If we worship power, recognition and fame, we'll never feel we have enough."[7] We need to recover our own tradition. If we want our children to be happy and thrive, we simply need to excavate what we already have.

---

[5] Benedict XVI, "Address of the Holy Father to Pupils."

[6] Rui Shi, Shilei Zhang, and Danmin Miao, "Failure-Related Action Orientation and Life Satisfaction: The Mediating Role of Forgivingness," *Journal of Happiness Studies* Vol. 17, Issue 5 (Oct 2016): 1891–1903. https://doi.org/10.10 07/s10902-015-9676-y.

[7] Arianna Huffington, *Thrive: The Third Metric to Redefining Success and Creating a Life of Well-being, Wisdom, and Wonder* (London: Random House, 2014), 259.

So what does this mean in practice? First and foremost, it means a return to prayer. Mindfulness may have an occasional role to play in our schools, but we should be very wary of what is essentially secularized Buddhism. Some Catholics argue that mindfulness can be a helpful way of practically de-stressing, but there is a danger that, instead of mindfulness, we find that our students have succumbed to mefulness.[8] Instead of drawing on the doubtful spirituality of mindfulness we should focus instead on teaching our children how to pray, helping them to discover the riches of meditative prayer and the classics of Catholic spirituality. It is surely no coincidence that schools and individuals have turned to other sources of meditation at exactly the same time that silence and reverence have seeped away from so much liturgical practice. Rediscovering the richness of the liturgy can therefore be one step toward true happiness. Bishop Egan of Portsmouth has usefully spelt out some practical ideas in this area:

> We should focus on prayer and the spiritual development of pupils, and also of staff, who in some manner model it. Spiritual development can be offered to every student in school, regardless of affiliation. We might focus on interiority, an atmosphere in school at appropriate times of recollection. We could help pupils develop spiritual skills: meditation, contemplation, silent prayer, biblical prayer, spontaneous prayer. We could hold Eucharistic *Holy Half-Hours,* pay short visits to church, give formation in *lectio divina* and imaginative prayer. We could open the treasury of Catholic spirituality and the writings of the saints, inviting representatives from our diocesan religious communities: the Franciscans, Dominicans, Benedictines, Salesians. Staff need a programme, with formation-sessions and if possible, retreat-days. They might frequently

---

[8] See, for example, Roman Krznaric's criticism that "the popular secularised version of mindfulness—as opposed to the centuries-old Buddhist tradition—has ended up focusing too much on the self, leaving it thin on moral foundations." Roman Krznaric, *Carpe Diem Regained: The Vanishing Art of Seizing the Day* (London: Unbound, 2017), 124–25.

offer mission-prayers for the spread of the Gospel and the love of Jesus.[9]

If true happiness can only be found in God, then we need to help our children turn to God in prayer. What comes next? Since love of God naturally leads to love of neighbor, our prayer must naturally lead to acts of charity. In our self-obsessed age there is a real danger that we unwittingly encourage our students to think only about themselves by focusing exclusively on *their* needs and *their* problems. Catholic schools should instead have robust community service programs, serving the poor and the needy in their communities. Again, Bishop Egan offers helpful advice:

> Schools and parishes, alone or together, could undertake simple mission-projects. Parishes and schools could leaflet a new housing development, operate a food-bank, serve the poor, establish a stall on a local market, visit retirement homes, make use of social media, hand commuters invitations to a parish event, hold a Theology on Tap session in a local pub, organise special prayers and devotions, talk with people at the school gates, and so on. Doing a Catholic form of street witness—a procession, music, leafleting shops, praying the Rosary—can be a fruitful mission-project.[10]

We should not set up charity schemes solely in order to make our pupils happy, but that will be their effect.

Happiness lessons?

So where does this leave happiness lessons? Counterintuitively, if we put prayer and charity at the heart of our education system, we may be able to give *more* time to the sort of activities that currently constitute wellbeing programs, because they will be built on sound foundations. However, we also need to remember that if we are to transform our education system and transform our

---

[9] "The Future of Our Diocesan Schools."
[10] Ibid.

students, we need virtue education more than we need happiness programs.

If we are going to build up the cardinal virtues of temperance, prudence, justice and courage as well as the theological virtues of faith, hope and love, we need to ensure that the virtues are part and parcel of everyday life. Rather than restrict virtue education to occasional lessons or special days, we should instead embed it into the life of our schools.

Since relationships matter more than programs, we need to give teachers time to develop relationships with their students. A simple practical measure for schools would be to give teachers time each week with individual tutees. Just as parents need to waste time with their children, teachers need to give genuine time to their students if they want them to flourish.[11] What children need is us. What children need is God's love, the source of all true happiness, through us.

[11] As St Josemaria Escriva once said: "Parents should find time to spend with their children, to talk with them. They are the most important thing—more important than business or work or rest. In their conversations, parents should make an effort to listen, to pay attention, to understand, to recognize the fact that their children are sometimes partly right—or even completely right—in some of their rebellious attitudes." St Josemaria Escriva, "Questions About the Family," accessed October 24, 2017. http://www.josemariae-scriva.info/article/14-questions-about-the-family. See also Pope Francis, "The Family 3.—The Father," Vatican website, accessed October 24, 2017. https://w2.vatican.va/content/francesco/en/audiences/2015/documents/papa-franc esco_20150128_udienza-generale.html.

9

Winnie-the-Pooh Apps

A RESPECTED CHILDREN'S PUBLISHER recently launched a Winnie-the-Pooh smartphone app containing abridged versions of the A. A. Milne stories. According to the developer, "Today's children's attention spans are slightly different to how they were in 1926. We have a minute to get them on board. If not, they will move on to the next app. We have to make sure the story moves on at a good pace." The mind boggles at what A. A. Milne would have made of this, but, undeterred by that concern, the developer continues by saying that "one of the pitfalls of a very interactive experience is that children quickly learn that they can just swipe through the text to get to the next game, so we decided to opt for something subtle"—something "subtle" in this case being animations of E. H. Shepard's illustrations. To all which we might be tempted to respond: right problem, wrong solution. Instead of thoughtless swiping, maybe children should read the books.

Good books

Books do still matter, and good books matter more.[1] A British Headmaster, Andrew Halls, recently set a literary cat among the pigeons by writing in a *Sunday Times* blog about "bad" children's books, by which he meant "books that are so simplistic, brutal or

---

[1] The section that follows is adapted from Roy Peachey, "Book Boxes for Schools and Families," *The Universe Education Supplement*, September/October 2017, 16–17.

banal that they are barely worth reading," and the consequent importance of "good books" in the classroom.[2]

Raising the question of what sort of education we want for our children, Halls turned to the analogy of food. Why give our children "industrialised literary fast-food," he asked, when we could serve them the equivalent of slow food? Writing in the 18th century, St Alphonsus Liguori made a strikingly similar point: "St Basil was right to call books *the food of the soul*; because just as food is pleasurable while we eat it, and goes on to become human blood, so a book pleases when read—for who reads unwillingly?—and thus is more quickly digested."[3] If a book is good, St Alphonsus Liguori thought, the soul is truly fed, but if a book's contents do not promote the true, the beautiful and the good, the reader is in danger of developing something worse than indigestion, since "a reader gives himself like a student to the author he reads, offering him a docile and benevolent heart, and thus leaves himself vulnerable to deception."

St Alphonsus Liguori and Andrew Halls suggest different solutions to the problem of bad books, but both are clear about the fact that a solution is needed. We may not want (or be able) to ban harmful books completely, but we can certainly promote good ones. And there's the rub. With thousands of children's books being published each year, it is difficult to keep up. How can we possibly know which books are going to be food for our children's souls and which are going to create lasting damage?

Part of the answer is that we don't need to keep up. As I have already argued, there is a tendency in our culture to value only what is new and to dismiss what was produced even a few decades ago. This cult of the new has badly affected library services, with old stock being routinely sold off or discarded in favor

---

[2] Andrew Halls, "Why We're Weaning Pupils Off Literary Fast Food," *The Sunday Times Blog*, March 26, 2017, accessed October 24, 2017. https://www.kcs.org.uk/media/1062/2017_03_26-why-were-weaning-pupils-off-literary-fast-food.pdf.

[3] St Alphonsus Liguori, "On the Utility and Necessity of Prohibiting Harmful Books," *The Josias*, accessed October 24, 2017. https://thejosias.com/2015/07/22/on-the-utility-and-necessity-of-prohibiting-harmful-books.

of the newest examples of literary fast-food. But what are we losing in the process? We are losing books by great children's authors like Hilda van Stockum, for a start. Van Stockum is scarcely a household name, but she should be. Born in the Netherlands (where her most famous book, *The Winged Watchman*, is set), she also lived in Ireland (where her *Bantry Bay* series is based) and the USA (where the wonderful *Mitchells* series begins). She wrote superb books for varying age groups in a wide range of styles, yet you will struggle to find any of her books in most public or school libraries.

If we want our children to read good books like these, we may need to take matters into our own hands. We can start by creating the sort of book boxes that Andrew Halls remembers from his youth. His English teacher "had a scruffy box of books and challenged us to read every book in it—all chosen by him. I guess there were 40 or 50. I was competitive, so I read all of them." These book boxes may sit in every English classroom, but we may also create our own boxes at home. And if we don't have 40 or 50 good books to hand, we can buy or rescue the old books that librarians have offloaded.

Of course, some people will argue that I am being hopelessly naïve. Children today simply will not read old books. The language is too difficult and the covers are not glossy enough. If that really is the case, then we need to introduce a new diet gradually. C.S. Lewis suggested, in his introduction to St Athanasius' *On the Incarnation*, that "it is a good rule, after reading a new book, never to allow yourself another new one till you have read an old one in between. If that is too much for you, you should at least read one old one to every three new ones."[4] Wise advice indeed.

So which books should we include in our boxes? We should certainly not limit ourselves to fiction. Biographies like *Road to Valor* by Aili and Andres McConnon and autobiographical works like *The Bells of Nagasaki* by Takashi Nagai would be great for teenagers, while the *Uncle Albert* books by Russell Stannard and imaginative reconstructions of actual events like *What if They Find Us?* by Kathy Clark or any of the Vision Books from Ignatius

---

[4] Lewis, *St Athanasius on the Incarnation*, 4.

Press work well for younger students. Graphic novels also have their place. The *Loupio* books by Jean-François Kieffer are wonderful introductions to St Francis for young children, while Simone Lia's *Please God, Find Me a Husband* is aimed at teenagers and young adults.

Some contemporary fiction can also be recommended. Kyung-Sook Shin's *Please Look After Mother* and Tim Gautreaux's *Waiting for the Evening News* are excellent books for older students, but there are many good novels for younger children too, including *The Gospel Time Trekker* series by Sr Maria Grace Dateno and Frank Cottrell Boyce's *Chitty Chitty Bang Bang* sequels. What is special about these books is that, drawing on Ian Fleming's original book rather than on Roald Dahl's dark screenplay, they feature a family having an adventure together.

There is a great deal to be said for Great Books programs, but good books come first. In fact, good books can lead us onto great ones. That is another reason why we should not neglect old books. Anything by George MacDonald, Andrew Lang, Laura Ingalls Wilder or Roger Lancelyn Green, for example, is worth reading. Simply because an author has been largely forgotten—as the example of Hilda van Stockum should remind us—does not mean that his or her books no longer have value.

Good children's books can lead us onto great books like *The Iliad*, St Augustine's *Confessions*, Dante's *Divine Comedy* and Chrétien de Troyes' *Arthurian Legends*. If we have books like these in our boxes, we may be able to ignite a love of great literature in students for whom the classics have always been, quite literally, a closed book. As C.S. Lewis pointed out,

> if the average student wants to find out something about Platonism, the very last thing he thinks of doing is to take a translation of Plato off the library shelf and read the *Symposium*. . . . The student is half afraid to meet one of the great philosophers face to face. He feels himself inadequate and thinks he will not understand him. But if he only knew, the great man, just because of his greatness, is much more intelligible than his modern commentator. . . . It has always therefore been one of my

main endeavors as a teacher to persuade the young that first-hand knowledge is not only more worth acquiring than second-hand knowledge, but is usually much easier and more delightful to acquire.[5]

Our book boxes need to contain both the new and the old, but, more importantly, they need to contain the great and the good. If we take a stand against bad books and actively promote the good, we might surprise our children with beauty, truth and goodness—especially if we help each other. There is no reason why schools and parents cannot swap ideas and families cannot swap books. Literary fast food will never feed our children's souls, so let's not settle for second best. There are plenty of good books out there: we don't need to turn to Winnie-the-Pooh apps instead.

Identifying the problem

Good books are the most obvious solution to bad apps, but we need to explore further. What are the problems associated with technology in our homes and schools today, and what are the possible solutions?

Here is one well-informed commentator setting out his views in an interview with *Wired* in 1996: "We live in an information economy, but I don't believe we live in an information *society.* People are thinking less than they used to. It's primarily because of television. People are reading less and they're certainly thinking less. So, I don't see most people using the Web to get more information. We're already in information overload. No matter how much information the Web can dish out, most people get far more information than they can assimilate anyway."[6]

Who was this commentator who claimed that people are thinking less and reading less? Who was this Luddite who blamed

---

[5] Lewis, *St Athanasius on the Incarnation*, 3.

[6] "Steve Jobs: A Wired Life—The next insanely great thing," *Wired*, December 2011, accessed October 24, 2017. http://www.wired.co.uk/article/the-next-insanely-great-thing.

TV and pointed out the limits of the internet? Who was this backward-looking technophobe who in the same interview argued that "What's wrong with education cannot be fixed with technology"?

It was none other than Steve Jobs.

And if you are wondering whether Steve Jobs was a lone voice in Silicon Valley, then take a look at this excerpt from *The New York Times*:

> LOS ALTOS, California.—The chief technology officer of eBay sends his children to a nine-classroom school here. So do employees of Silicon Valley giants like Google, Apple, Yahoo and Hewlett-Packard.
>
> But the school's chief teaching tools are anything but high-tech: pens and paper, knitting needles and, occasionally, mud. Not a computer to be found. No screens at all. They are not allowed in the classroom, and the school even frowns on their use at home.[7]

It's like using toothpaste

What reason do media high-fliers like Alan Eagle, who works for Google, give for sending their children to this virtually technology-free Waldorf School? "I fundamentally reject the notion you need technology aids in grammar school," he said. "The idea that an app on an iPad can better teach my kids to read or do arithmetic, that's ridiculous."

He argues that picking up computer skills is "supereasy. It's like learning to use toothpaste. At Google and all these places, we make technology as brain-dead easy to use as possible. There's no reason why kids can't figure it out when they get older."

So let me set out my stall here. I am not arguing that we should necessarily remove electronic media from our schools and

---

[7] Matt Richtel, "A Silicon Valley School That Doesn't Compute," *New York Times*, October 22, 2011, accessed October 24, 2017. http://www.nytimes.com/2011/10/23/technology/at-waldorf-school-in-silicon-valley-technology-can-wait.html.

homes. I am arguing that the electronic media should be kept firmly in its place, because, like Steve Jobs, I believe that what's wrong with education cannot be fixed with technology. Clearly we all depend, to a greater or lesser extent, on technology. Clearly our children are going to be growing up in a world where they need to be technologically adept. But it is also clear that in the great technological rush, we are accumulating all sorts of problems for ourselves and our children, not least of which is the loss of basic skills—the scaffolding on which technology relies.

I was speaking recently to a British space scientist, an amazing man whose work revolves around taking the very latest in technological innovations—often innovations developed by mobile phone companies—adapting them in his laboratory and launching them into space as micro-satellites. The students with whom he works are media- and technology-savvy. It's a success story from beginning to end—or so it seems. "Are there any problems?" I asked. "Yes," he replied, "we have to run remedial maths classes because the students' basic skills aren't any longer up to scratch."

I do not deny the benefits that technology brings, but just as I believe that certain books are suitable for 11-year-olds and certain books aren't, I also believe that certain technologies are appropriate for certain age groups and that we need to work hard to stop the drift toward dependency on electronic media. This is not a negative aspiration, because our main task as educators is not technological. Our duty is to help children develop the virtues so that they can make the most of their God-given skills. Once they have developed these skills and virtues, once they have developed powers of discernment and discrimination, then they will be able to make wise technological decisions. Hopefully, they will master the electronic media, rather than be mastered by the latest products and the marketing campaigns that accompany them.

Twelve-and-a-half years of your life

If there is any doubt about the scale of the problem, let's look at some statistics.

In the USA, tweens (8–12 year olds) use screen media for more than four and a half hours a day, and teenagers average six hours and forty minutes a day.

51% of teenagers watch TV while doing their homework, 50% use social media while doing their homework, and 60% text while doing their homework. Most of these children say that "multitasking" in this way does not affect the quality of their work.

53% of tweens have their own tablets and 67% of teenagers have their own smartphones, while 47% of tweens and 57% of teenagers have TVs in their rooms.[8]

In the UK, 20% of 3–4 year olds have a TV in their bedroom. But they also spend an average of eight hours and eighteen minutes a week online.[9]

The amount of time children spend online changes each year, as does the amount of time they spend on different types of device. In general, the trend is away from TV and toward online media. Precise figures change rapidly in this field, but the overall message is very clear. If children have electronic devices in their bedrooms, including mobile phones and other internet-enabled devices as well as TVs, parental influence is inevitably impaired. If children spend four hours a day online or watching TV, then the parent's voice is dulled.

According to psychologist Aric Sigman, the average 6-year-old has watched TV for nearly one full year of his or her short life. By the age of 75, people will, on average, have watched twelve and a half years of TV. That is twelve and a half years of 24 hours a day. If we work on the basis that we need to sleep sometimes, we can say that the average person will have lost 25 years of his or her life to TV by the time he gets to the age of 75.

No wonder then that Sigman ends his book, *Remotely Controlled: How Television is Damaging Our Lives* with the question: "if

---

[8] "The Common Sense Census: Media Use by Tweens and Teens," Common Sense Media, 2015, accessed October 24, 2017, https://www.commonsensemedia.org/sites/default/files/uploads/research/census_researchreport.pdf.

[9] "Children and Parents: Media Use and Attitudes Report," Ofcom, November 2016, accessed October 24, 2017, https://www.ofcom.org.uk/__data/assets/pdf_file/0034/93976/Children-Parents-Media-Use-Attitudes-Report-2016.pdf.

you were on your deathbed and someone could give you back those missing twelve-and-a-half years to be with people you loved, and maybe do things differently, would you take their offer? Or would you say, 'No, thanks. I'm glad I spent that time watching TV'?"[10]

Less journalistically, he argues in an article for *Archives of Disease in Childhood* that "irrespective of the content or educational value of what is being viewed, the sheer amount of average daily screen time during discretionary hours after school is increasingly being considered an independent risk factor for disease."[11] Spending that amount of time in front of a screen, whether it is a TV, phone or computer screen, simply isn't good for us.

The obvious solution is to limit screen time. Sigman suggests the following RDA, or Recommended Daily Allowance:

• Children under three should see no screen entertainment.

• After this age, television viewing of good quality programs should be limited to *an hour a day.*

• Teenagers should be limited to one-and-a-half hours a day.

• And for adults, two hours a day.

The problem here, as we all know, is that wills weaken when we are tired, so another solution is simply not to have a TV at all. I realize that making such a suggestion immediately makes me a social outcast, but I'm amazed more people don't take up this option. I don't underestimate the scale of the challenge. One academic study into the effects of a TV turn-off week in the US reported that "the first 3 or 4 days for most persons were the worst, even in many homes where viewing was minimal and where there were other ongoing activities. In over half of all the

---

[10] Aric Sigman, *Remotely Controlled: How Television is Damaging Our Lives* (London: Vermilion, 2005), 328.

[11] Aric Sigman, "Time for a View on Screen Time," *Archives of Disease in Childhood* 97 (2012): 935.

households, during these first few days of loss, the regular routines were disrupted, family members had difficulties in dealing with the newly available time, anxiety and aggressions were expressed." But, and this is the hopeful part, "By the second week, a move toward adaptation to the situation was common."[12]

The internet and technological promiscuity

However, the problems presented by television pale into relative insignificance when compared with the difficulties presented by the internet and by what Ofcom misleadingly calls "multi-tasking" and what Sherry Turkle, Professor of the Social Studies of Science and Technology at MIT, calls "technological promiscuity."[13] Let's be clear what we're talking about here: it isn't the sort of multi-tasking my wife does so well. It's texting while watching TV. It's Skyping and typing at the same time. It's children being on Facebook while doing their English homework.

There are essentially two problems here. The first is that "we expect more from technology and less from each other," as Sherry Turkle puts it. Authentic communication is replaced by the illusion of companionship that comes from being online. The more we and our children use smartphones and social networks and the more we play games online, text, browse and watch TV, the less time we spend with each other. The second problem is what Nicholas Carr, in *The Shallows: How the Internet is Changing the Way We Think, Read and Remember*, calls "the constant distractedness that the Net encourages."[14] This is a massive issue for schools. Perhaps the single most important academic attribute teachers can encourage children to develop is the power of intense, focused concentration. The problem, as Carr explains

---

[12] Robert Kubey, "Television Dependence, Diagnosis, and Prevention: With Commentary on Video Games, Pornography, and Media Education," in *Tuning In To Young Viewers: Social Science Perspectives on Television*, ed. Tannis M. MacBeth (London: Sage, 1996), 231.

[13] Sherry Turkle, *Alone Together* (New York: Basic Books, 2012), 10.

[14] Nicholas Carr, *The Shallows: How the Internet is Changing the Way We Think, Read and Remember* (London: Atlantic Books, 2010), 119.

brilliantly in his book, is that the very nature of the internet is working against us: "the Net seizes our attention only to scatter it."[15]

As Marshall McLuhan, a devout Catholic, daily communicant and media personality, showed many years ago, technology can never be neutral. The medium is the message.[16] McLuhan's insight has only become clearer since the invention and spread of the internet. "Dozens of studies by psychologists, neurobiologists, educators, and Web designers," Nicholas Carr writes, "point to the same conclusion: when we go online, we enter an environment that promotes cursory reading, hurried and distracted thinking, and superficial learning. It's possible to think deeply while surfing the Net, just as it's possible to think shallowly while reading a book, but that's not the type of thinking the technology encourages and rewards."[17] Young children no longer have the ability to concentrate on *Winnie-the-Pooh* stories (a serious enough problem in its own right), but the problems certainly don't stop there. Since the "key to memory consolidation is attentiveness," and since the internet seizes our attention only to scatter it, it should not surprise us that internet use atrophies the memory, and this matters because our memory is not an external hard drive: "With each expansion of our memory comes an enlargement of our intelligence."[18]

We need to insist time and time again that electronic media are not blunt tools. The internet is never neutral. Books, magazines, and newspapers have all changed because of the Net. Sentences are shorter. Hyperlinks are essential. Multimedia content displaces text. In other words, our children face more distractions and more dumbing down. But, as Nicholas Carr again explains: "Even people who are wary of the Net's ever-expanding influence rarely allow their concerns to get in the way of their use and enjoyment of the technology. . . . The computer screen bulldozes

---

[15] Ibid., 118.

[16] Marshall McLuhan, *The Medium Is the Massage: An Inventory of Effects* (Berkeley, CA: Gingko Press, 2013).

[17] Carr, *The Shallows*, 115–16.

[18] Ibid., 192.

our doubts with its bounties and conveniences. It is so much our servant that it would seem churlish to notice that it is also our master."[19]

That is why we need to make a determined effort to take control of the internet connection. Wifi can be switched off: it doesn't have to stay on 24 hours a day. Similarly, cell phones don't have to be carried everywhere: if children have a cell phone for security reasons, there is no reason why they should not leave it on the hall table every time they come in. Another solution is to ration the use of internet-enabled devices, and that means parents checking that they know which of their children's devices are internet-enabled. Karl Hopwood of esafety Ltd reports that many parents assure him that their children don't have the internet in their rooms because they don't have computers in their rooms, without realizing that their children's games consoles and other devices are hooked up to the worldwide web.

We cannot forget the many benefits that the internet brings: internet shopping; contact with friends and family in other countries; instant information. But it is precisely because the internet brings benefits that it blinds us to other fundamental problems. We all know that children need to be protected from much of the content they are exposed to online, but it is not the terrible stuff that is pumped into our homes by the internet that is the real problem. The real problem is the way the internet shapes the way we read, think and learn: "media aren't just channels of information," Nicholas Carr writes. "They supply the stuff of thought, but they also shape the process of thought. And what the Net seems to be doing is chipping away at my capacity for concentration and contemplation. Whether I'm online or not, my mind now expects to take in information the way the Net distributes it: in a swiftly moving stream of particles. Once I was a scuba diver in the sea of words. Now I zip along the surface like a guy on a Jet Ski."[20]

---

[19] Ibid., 4.
[20] Ibid., 6–7.

George Orwell's radio

It is easy to dismiss technological warnings as the ramblings of unworldly Luddites. This is why writers like Nicholas Carr, Neil Postman, and Sherry Turkle are so important: they're not dropouts from society. They are technological insiders, and what they see from the inside makes them want to sound the alarm bells. So before we consider some very practical proposals for school and home, let me deal with a few more possible objections to what I've been arguing. A very commonly-heard argument is that new technology always provokes fears and that, after a while, we adjust. We get used to what had scared us with its very novelty. Think about George Orwell's warnings about the radio, they say.

So let's look at what Orwell actually said: "The whole trend of the age is away from creative communal amusements and towards solitary mechanical ones. The pub, with its elaborate social ritual, its animated conversations . . . is gradually [being] replaced by the passive, drug-like pleasures of the cinema and the radio."[21] That was in 1943, and it sounds remarkably prescient to me.

He returned to the same theme in 1946, and I challenge you to replace "radio" with "MP3 player" or "TV" and see if what he said then still holds true now:

> In very many English homes the radio is literally never turned off, though it is manipulated from time to time so as to make sure that only light music will come out of it. I know people who will keep the radio playing all through a meal and at the same time continue talking just loudly enough for the voices and the music to cancel out. This is done with a definite purpose. The music prevents the conversation from becoming serious or even coherent.[22]

Some people might complain that I am picking unfairly on electronic media. To those people I would say that the internet

---

[21] George Orwell, "Review of The Pub and The People by Mass-Observation," The Orwell Foundation, accessed October 24, 2017. https://www.orwellfoundation.com/the-orwell-foundation/orwell/essays-and-other-works/review-of-the-pub-and-the-people-by-mass-observation.

[22] George Orwell, "Pleasure Spots," *Tribune*, January 11, 1946.

has taken us into new, more worrying, territory, but I would also agree that the print media are a problem. As C. John Somerville, Professor Emeritus of History at the University of Florida, puts it in one of his books:

> Newspapers and books are both printed, to be sure, but they are not the same in their effect. Newspapers are the opposite of books, taking things apart rather than putting them together. You must disassemble reality if you want to make a business of selling information. There must be a new issue or broadcast every day, whether or not the world has turned a corner. Even if journalists are following an old story, they must go a new direction with it each day. If they can't, they must switch our attention to something else.[23]

He also points out that one of the top liberal arts colleges in the USA "used to tell the students it accepted to read the *Washington Post* all summer before they arrived, when they had all the world's literature to choose from." We have choices and, given a choice, we might be better off reading a good book than leafing through a newspaper.

Another objection is that technology can provide answers to specific educational issues such as dyslexia. I do not deny that there may be a place for computers in an individual education plan, but this is what the authors of a recent book about teaching literacy to learners with dyslexia think: "fluent handwriting remains particularly important for learners with spelling difficulties, especially those with dyslexia, because it helps establish motor co-ordination and memory. . . . A continuous cursive handwriting style . . . helps learners to gain automatically in both handwriting and spelling. There is no strong evidence as yet that word-processing helps in the same way."[24]

---

[23] C. John Somerville, *The Decline of the Secular University* (New York: Oxford University Press, 2006), 138. See also Postman, *Amusing Ourselves to Death*.

[24] Kathleen Kelly and Sylvia Phillips, *Teaching Literacy to Learners with Dyslexia: A Multi-sensory Approach* (London: Sage, 2011), 81–82.

The final objection I am going to deal with is a much more pragmatic one: what I have said may be true, but we live in the 21st century, and so there is no way we can possibly live without electronic media. There is some truth in this objection, though there are still plenty of people who manage to function without a television, a mobile phone, or any form of social networking. I would even argue that it is possible to achieve a huge amount more than we might think without the internet. I was somewhat taken aback to discover, for example, that when Norman Davies was researching his 1000-page *Europe: A History,* his favored resource was not the internet but his 1911 edition of the *Encyclopedia Britannica.* But what I would say, above all else, is that children don't need these distractions now. While they are learning and growing they need the best we can give them, not the shallow pleasures of the electronic media. And if they don't have these distractions, we can better prepare them for the world into which they will graduate.

Some practical apps

So what, practically speaking, can we do in our schools and homes? First and foremost, we ought to keep in mind that fundamental idea that schools should learn from homes, not the other way round. Only in the most dysfunctional families would email or text be the main means of communication, yet we can easily allow ourselves to slip into that pattern in our schools and workplaces. In fact, we might go further and suggest that we need to keep our schools small, so that face-to-face communication remains the norm. Small is still beautiful.[25] We should also design our schools so that straightforward human relationships take precedence over faceless interaction. Do we have places where teachers can meet and chat, or do we hide behind departmental office walls? Are there places where students can talk to individual teachers, or are our buildings designed only for crowds? Above all else, we should always insist that technology serves us, rather

---

[25] E. F. Schumacher, *Small is Beautiful* (London: Abacus, 1987).

than the other way round. What that means in practice will vary from institution to institution, but if we start by teaching etiquette, we will not go far wrong wherever we are. So here are some lessons we could teach our children:

- Face-to-face communication always comes first. When other people are in the room, they come first, not what is on the phone, tablet or computer screen.

- Phones do not always have to be answered or checked immediately.

- Immediate responses to emails should not be expected or demanded. It is often best to draft an email and to send it later.

- Emails should never be sent when the writer is annoyed or irritated.

- The same rules of English apply to emails as to letters. In particular, capitalization and punctuation should be used correctly, text abbreviations are not acceptable, and emails should always be signed.

- When listening to music through earphones, you should ensure that your music (or its bass line) cannot be heard by anyone else.

Then we could address some of the particular issues that we face in the classroom:

- Handwriting, rather than word-processing, should be the usual way of presenting work.

- Computers (and especially the internet) should not usually be required for homework. An internet-enabled computer should only be needed if there really is no other way of completing a particular piece of work, and this should be made clear by the teacher.

- Mobile phones should not be used during the school day.

• Children should not listen to music on any device while working (though a teacher may choose to play music for a particular exercise).

• As far as possible, work done on the computer should consist of real tasks: for example, learning coding rather than adding pictures to a Word document. (If you are producing a school magazine, it makes sense to use editorial software, but there is no need to use it for anachronistic newspaper front pages in history—"The Daily Tudor Breaking News: Henry VIII Divorces Again.")

• Children should be taught how to stay safe online and should receive age-appropriate advice.

• Children should be given practical advice about privacy settings and similar issues.

• Children should be taught about plagiarism and how to assess the relevance, validity and believability of all documents, whether they are found in books or online.

• Children should be taught research skills and how to reference what they have found.

Lastly, we should ensure that what we lay down for our students also applies to us. It is not uncommon for teachers to be tied to their screens—either because they are overwhelmed by the daily barrage of emails or because they cannot break the habit—while the school is encouraging its students to break free. With that in mind, here are my suggestions for schools and teachers:

• Emails should be the communication of last resort and should not be checked or sent after an agreed time. Sundays should be entirely email-free.

• Teachers should not use their cell phones in public spaces during the school day.

• Teachers should model the behavior they hope for in their students. That means teachers should be encouraged to read, spend time outside, and put their marking away whenever possible.

So there we are. After all that, I feel the need for a break. I think I'll go and read a book. In fact, I'm going to read *Winnie-the-Pooh* and see whether I can still concentrate all the way to the end.

PART THREE

Transformations

10

Slow Education

WE ALL KNOW the challenges we face today, so how do we ensure that we are not swamped by hopelessness? How do we transform Catholic education so that it can transform our children's lives? We may need to begin by acknowledging that, in our secular age, we cannot expect to build a Catholic society. Rather, it is the strength of our Catholic counter-culture that is now the measure of our success. That is why, in this section of the book, I focus on what kind of counter-culture we might want to build in our homes, schools and colleges, and the practical changes we need to implement if we are to bring about great change.

Building a counter-culture rather than shaping the culture should not be thought of as an admission of defeat. Instead, it is a recognition that we are poor banished children of Eve and that, in this our exile, our task is to build the City of God rather than the culture of the world. We still need to think big. We still have a massive task on our hands. If we are going to make a difference to Catholic education, we need to do more than tinker around the edges.

A useful starting point when thinking about practical change is the concept of slow education. The slow movement is often misunderstood, so it is important to clarify what I mean here. The slow movement began with slow food, which was itself a response to the opening of a McDonald's in Rome. It was a reaction against the homogenization of society and expressed itself through a defense of local food and local cuisine. It drew upon an understanding of time that wasn't shaped by modern, post-industrial society.

Languages and music

Slow education also starts with a recognition that how we regard time and how we respond to it matters, because true learning, deep learning, takes time. A lecturer in the department of Asian and Middle Eastern Studies at the University of Cambridge once told me that the question she is most often asked is, "How long did it take you to learn Chinese?" Her reply to this unanswerable question was always "I don't know, because I'm still learning."

Much the same could be said of music. Like many parents, I would like my children to learn an instrument, but I know there can be no instant gratification here. If they are going to play Bach's Preludes and Fugues in the future then I am going to have to put up with Twinkle Twinkle Little Star now. Unfortunately, one of the difficulties we face in education is that instant gratification has been institutionalized. The message of countless TV shows is that instant fame is possible as long as you've got talent. But that is an institutional lie: what actually matters is graft, and graft takes time.

Planes and poetry

I came across a great example of this when I visited St Paul's Convent School in Hong Kong. On display in the entrance hall was a cardboard plane. Why? Because students at the school, with a little help from a parent who was in the business, built a plane—a real plane. It took them seven years. It flew. It stayed up. It came down safely. But it took them seven years. Many of the students who worked on the plane had left school before it had its maiden flight, but even so, they knew that they had worked on something special, a project that could not be rushed.

Not many students will have the chance to build a plane, but many are asked to write creatively. Our usual approach, as teachers, is to have a lesson, set some homework and then expect a worthwhile piece of writing to emerge, but that's not how writing works. Charles Causley, who was both a fantastic poet and a primary schoolteacher, used to give his pupils a year in which to write their poems because that's how long poetry takes, a fact that was brought home to me when I bumped into a friend who is a published poet on the last day of his holiday and the first day of mine.

"Have you had a good week?" I asked.

"It's been wonderful," he replied.

"Have you written any poetry while you've been here?"

"Oh yes, it's been a productive week. I've written three lines."

We all know that learning languages, writing poetry, and building planes take time. We know that true learning cannot be rushed, but, usually because of institutional pressures, we feel the need for speed. However, if we are to transform Catholic education, these are the pressures we need to resist. Rome was not built in a day and knowledge cannot be mastered in a day either.

Result-driven demands may be built into the post-industrial model of education, but there are counter-pressures—not least because the pace of education causes, or at least contributes to, obvious social and personal problems. Anorexia, bulimia, depression, anxiety and stress are part and parcel of many contemporary schools, so it's no surprise that parents are on the lookout for an alternative approach. That is why the recent surge of interest in forest schools is hardly a surprise.

Maria Montessori and Forest Schools

I have already written about Forest Schools in the context of embodied education, but, crucially, there is more to Forest Schools than outdoor education. The first principle of a Forest School education, which normally complements mainstream education, is as follows: "Forest School is a long-term process of frequent and regular sessions in a woodland or natural environment, rather than a one-off visit."[1] In other words, Forest Schools are not only a reaction against the cooping up of children that has become such a pervasive aspect of modern life; they are also a response to a vague unease about the pace of education. What

[1] "Good Practice," Forest School Association, accessed October 24, 2017. http://www.forestschoolassociation.org/full-principles-and-criteria-for-good-practice.

Forest Schools offer is education that responds to the seasons, taking circadian rhythms, both ours and nature's, seriously. Forest Schools are not an isolated example: Christian educators from Charlotte Mason to Maria Montessori have attempted to rejig education by encouraging us to step back from the frantic rush of the mainstream. Montessori schools in particular are built on the principles of slow education, though Maria Montessori, who was a devout Catholic, came up with her approach long before Carlo Petrini launched his assault on McDonald's:

> Little children accomplish slowly and perseveringly various complicated operations agreeable to them, such as dressing, undressing, cleaning the room, washing themselves, setting the table, eating, etc. In all this they are extremely patient, overcoming all the difficulties presented by an organism still in process of formation. But we, on the other hand, noticing that they are 'tiring themselves out' or 'wasting time' in accomplishing something which we would do in a moment and without the least effort, put ourselves in the child's place and do it ourselves. Always with the same erroneous idea, that the end to be obtained is the completion of the action, we dress and wash the child, we snatch out of his hands objects which he loves to handle, we pour the soup into his bowl, we feed him, we set the table for him. And after such services, we consider him, with that injustice always practiced by those who domineer over others even with benevolent intentions, to be incapable and inept. We often speak of him as 'impatient' simply because we are not patient enough to allow his actions to follow laws of time differing from our own; we call him 'tyrannical' exactly because we employ tyranny towards him. This stain, this false imputation, this calumny on childhood has become an integral part of the theories concerning childhood, in reality so patient and gentle.[2]

[2] Maria Montessori, *The Montessori Method* (New York: Frederick A. Stokes, 1912), 358–59.

When our children are first born, we accept that our lives have to run at a different pace. We accept (sometimes grudgingly, I admit) that we will lose sleep, that babies need regular feeds, that we can no longer lead the lives we led before. But it isn't long before we attempt to reestablish the pattern we had in place before we had children, expecting children to do whatever needs to be done in timeframes we construct. How many family arguments are caused because parents and children work with different conceptions of time? I am not arguing that parents should capitulate in the face of teenage demands to lie in until mid-afternoon, nor am I suggesting that we abandon all attempts to arrive on time for Mass, school or any other activity, but I am suggesting that we recognize our own obsession with time for what it is: a deeply ingrained habit that may not always work well for us or our children.

The formal logic of the clock

Changing our attitude toward time is difficult, but most of us share a nagging feeling that change is required. It wasn't just W.H. Auden who believed that "All our intuitions mock / the formal logic of the clock."[3] Fortunately for us, we can now see that Auden's intuitions were more than just that: they were grounded in the structure of reality. In *Elogio della lentezza*—a book that has been translated into several different languages, but, tellingly, not into English—Lamberto Maffei, an eminent Italian professor of neurobiology, argues that education has to be slow because it must respond to the biological reality of child development.[4] Maffei points out that one of the striking differences between humans and other animals is the length of our childhood, the sheer amount of time it takes us to develop. He also reminds us

[3] W.H. Auden, "New Year Letter," in *Collected Longer Poems* (London: Faber and Faber, 1968), 92.
[4] Lamberto Maffei, *Elogio della lentezza* (Bologna: Il mulino, 2014). Translated into French as Lamberto Maffei, *Hâte-toi lentement: sommes-nous programmés pour la vitesse du monde numérique?* trans. Lucia Di Bisceglie with Camille Zabka (Limoges: Fyp éditions, 2016).

that the brain works in two distinct ways: there is a rapid response system—the classic "fight or flight response" of a thousand pop psychology talks—and a reflective mode that is much more efficient and creative. Schools and businesses are often built on the assumption that we need to react quickly to external stimuli, but the brain does not work well—or, at least, it has limited utility—when responding to stress. True creation of any kind takes time, as Maffei shows by quoting French Mathematician Jacques Hadamard on the three stages of mathematical creation: preparation, incubation and illumination.

We can move quickly when we need to—we can have brainwaves and sudden insights—but only if we have slowly prepared the ground first. We can dash off a report or an essay, but only if we have already done the slow intellectual work. That is why Alexis de Tocqueville wrote that "nothing is more necessary to the cultivation of the advanced sciences or the elevated portion of the sciences than meditation."[5] From a neurobiological perspective, it is only when the brain is given the time it needs that it is capable of producing great work. The logic of the clock does not do justice to the way our minds really work, which is why slow education shouldn't be a bolt on to mainstream education, but an essential component of it.

We can see this by looking at almost any area of human endeavor. When Mozart was sixteen, for example, he traveled to Italy for the premiere of one of his operas, an opera he hadn't yet finished writing. So what did he do on the journey? He dashed off a great string quartet. What this story is generally used to illustrate, besides Mozart's youthful insouciance, is the importance of genius, but one of Mozart's letters suggests an application to the need for education to be slow: "When I am, so to speak, completely myself, completely alone and in a good humor, say traveling in a carriage or walking after a good meal, or during the night when I can't sleep, it is on these occasions that my ideas really

---

[5] Quoted in Matthew B. Crawford, "The Computerized Academy," *The New Atlantis*, accessed October 24, 2017. http://www.thenewatlantis.com/publications/the-computerized-academy.

flow. I don't know where they come from or how they arrive and I can't force them."[6] Even Mozart needed preparation and incubation before illumination came. And when it came, he had to write it down, even if he did have an operatic deadline looming.

Mozart and latent anxiety

Neurobiology and Mozart might seem a little distant from the reality of a class of restive teenagers, but looking at the biological underpinning of slow education helps us answer one of the obvious objections to these calls for change: namely, that slow education is all very well in an ideal world but it doesn't prepare today's students for the fast-paced world of deadlines and demands they will face when they graduate. The problem with such an objection is that it doesn't actually resolve the problem it is attempting to address. To the skeptics, I would argue that the beauty of slow education is that it prepares students for both a fast-paced and a slow-paced existence because it offers them a way to focus on what really matters.

Slow education is, and has to be, a great deal more than simply giving more time to activities like building planes and writing poetry. It is about providing the means by which students can work with real attention. In *Leisure, the Basis of Culture*, Josef Pieper quotes Richard Wright's observation that "latent anxiety" is "the mark of the world of work."[7] Latent anxiety, I would add, also characterizes the world of education, and latent anxiety kills creative thought. Without creative thought, students will not be able to flourish in the fast-paced world they are going to find when they graduate.

Latent anxiety can be generated from many sources, including the dominant model of time that has emerged from what Pieper calls a world of "total work"—time as economic principal. In the 19th century, we started to worry that we were wasting time. In

[6] Quoted in Maffei, *Hâte-toi lentement*, 138. My translation.
[7] Pieper, *Leisure, the Basis of Culture*, 51.

the 20th century, we began to manage it. Now, in the 21st century, we are overwhelmed by it. If we are to create real change in the education we offer our children, we need to recover a different understanding of time, one that would have been recognized by St Augustine and the Venerable Bede. We need to take seriously what Jacques Austerlitz says in W.G. Sebald's novel: "Time . . . was by far the most artificial of all our inventions, and in being bound to the planet turning on its own axis was no less arbitrary than would be, say, a calculation based on the growth of trees or the duration required for a piece of limestone to disintegrate."[8] Maybe one of the tasks of Catholic educators is to remind us of this simple fact.

Novels and ponds

Maybe good literature can do the same. Eugene Vodolazkin's *Laurus* is a novel about a healer and a holy fool in 15th-century Russia. As Laurus moves toward sanctity, time becomes increasingly liturgical, seasonal and cyclical, and, in passages of great lyrical beauty, different characters explain how he might escape the immanent frame entirely through this renewed (and lived) appreciation of time. But it is not just Laurus who escapes time: the novel does, too. As one character from 20th-century Leningrad explains,

> "Historians in the Middle Ages were unlike historians these days. They always looked for moral reasons as an explanation for historical events. It's like they didn't notice the direct connection between events. Or didn't attach much significance to it."

> "But how can you explain the world without seeing the connections?" said Alexandra, surprised.

> "They were looking above the everyday and seeing higher connections. Besides, time connected all events,

---

[8] W.G. Sebald, *Austerlitz* (London: Hamish Hamilton, 2001), 141–42.

even though people didn't consider that connection reliable."[9]

It is this "medieval" understanding of time that drives the novel. Why is this important? Because we need to get away from the idea that time runs at a fixed pace and that slow education is all about ignoring that reality.[10] Rather, slow education can help us recover a richer sense of time—one that would have been very familiar in premodernity and that we have not entirely lost today.

A couple of years ago, we moved house and took possession of a slightly down-at-heel pond. Over time, we cleared it out, replanted it and hoped that it now looked less of an eyesore. A few months later, to our great surprise, we discovered that we had tadpoles. We hadn't noticed frogspawn, we hadn't consciously intended to create a frog-friendly zone, but there they were, and our children were delighted. We watched them develop, grow legs and hop out of the water. They were tiny, no bigger than a fingernail. My intuition was that seeing all of this was good for our children, but I had a nagging doubt about whether it was educational. We didn't follow it up with a project. We didn't write about what we saw. We just marveled.

But if there is more to time than industrial time, and if Pieper is right about the difference between *ratio* and *intellectus*, then my vague intuition was right. We didn't apply discursive, logical thought to our tadpoles, but *intellectus* certainly came into play. We were receptive, and so our understanding grew. However, we were only able to be receptive because we were slow. Replanting our pond took time. The changes in the pond took time. And, through spending time in the garden—growing vegetables, playing football, enjoying the changing seasons—we put ourselves in a position where we could notice the tadpoles in the first place and be receptive to them once we had noticed.[11]

[9] Eugene Vodolazkin, *Laurus*, trans. Lisa C. Hayden (London: Oneworld, 2015), 192–93.

[10] See Marshall McLuhan, *Understanding Media* (London: ARK, 1987), 145–56.

[11] For more on my pond, see Roy Peachey, "Fishing for Koi with an Afghan Veteran," *First Things*, March 6, 2017, accessed October 24, 2017. https://www.

I can still hear objections: spending time with kids in the garden won't help us in the real world, and looking at tadpoles won't make a blind bit of difference to education. This would be true if the purpose of education were the passing of exams. But, as I argued in Chapter 1, the real end of education is neither passing exams nor getting into college. The real aim of education is God. What was once recognized as the truth remains true: we were created to know, love, and serve God and to be happy with Him forever in Heaven, not to get into college and find a well-paid job.

Lectio Divina *and slow reading*

Another way of putting this is to say, with a former Headmaster of Ampleforth College, that the school's task is to prepare its students for death. I thought of this when I went to Ampleforth last Easter and listened to one of the monks talk about slow reading. He began his talk by speaking about slow soccer, a game designed for players of a certain age who still like to have a kick about but who are no longer fit enough to run around for ninety minutes. In slow soccer, running is banned. But then he moved on to *Lectio Divina*, or slow reading, which is quite different from slow soccer. Just as slow education is not a slimmed-down—or slowed down—version of education for those who can't keep up, neither is *Lectio Divina* a slow version of reading for those who have inexplicably failed to speed-read. *Lectio Divina* is the slow, meditative reading and re-reading of Scriptural texts. It is reading in order to listen. It is poles apart from the type of reading most of us do today.

Pope Benedict XVI once made a bold claim about *Lectio Divina*:

> the ancient tradition of *Lectio Divina*: the diligent reading
> of Sacred Scripture accompanied by prayer brings about
> that intimate dialogue in which the person reading hears

---

firstthings.com / web-exclusives / 2017 / 03 / fishing-for-koi-with-an-afghan-veteran.

God who is speaking, and in praying, responds to him with trusting openness of heart. If it is effectively promoted, this practice will bring to the Church—I am convinced of it—a new spiritual springtime.[12]

How *Lectio Divina* might effect such radical change was explained by another Ampleforth monk, Fr Gabriel Everitt, who argued that radical change starts with "something very practical, which may sound rather boring, a schoolroom task," namely St Benedict's injunction in his Rule that "in the time remaining after Vigils, those who need to learn some of the psalter or readings should study them." In his talk, he conjured up the following image:

generations of monks in the cloisters, in the nooks and the crannies of their monasteries and choirs, alone or maybe in groups (since copies of the Scriptures may have been hard to come by) muttering over the words of the psalms and the readings, as often enough quite painfully and slowly, they committed them to memory. The slowness and the repetition of the work, its necessary patience, is its point. It was not in itself an arcane or complicated process. It was just learning by heart.

For [the Benedictine monks], as for example for the Desert Fathers before them, the practice had an effect, almost certainly not self-conscious or deliberate. It was at a deeper level than the conscious. Reading became meditation (in the sense of murmuring, repeating, learning, chewing over) became prayer became contemplation: these are the traditional stages of *lectio divina*: lectio, meditatio, oratio, contemplatio. It was perhaps a bit too simple and apparently undramatic for later ages, who

[12] Benedict XVI, "Address of his Holiness Benedict XVI to the Participants in the International Congress Organized to Commemorate the 40th Anniversary of the Dogmatic Constitution on Divine Revelation 'Dei Verbum,'" Vatican website, accessed October 24, 2017. http://w2.vatican.va/content/benedict-xvi/en/speeches/2005/september/documents/hf_ben-xvi_spe_20050916_40-dei-verbum.html.

sought to make it more deliberate and conscious and to systematise it more, but the practice had an effect, which was to shape a culture.[13]

Here, then, is a way of reading that is rarely taught in schools. As an English teacher, I spend a lot of time encouraging my students to read. I guide them through the reading of the year's set texts, and I discuss what I have been reading myself. However, I have rarely been in an educational environment where students are encouraged to carry out the equivalent of *Lectio Divina*: to read out loud, memorize, understand and put into practice. Yet that is what the ancients thought reading meant.

How might we bring back this understanding and practice of reading today? One way is to start with *Lectio Divina* as both a good in its own right and as a useful model to follow. This is what is beginning to happen at Ampleforth College, where half the students have chosen to join *Lectio Divina* groups. Whether they are conscious of it or not, they are relearning the art of slow reading.[14]

Having rediscovered how to read, students need to be given the time to do so. Even in establishments that place a high value on reading the great books, there can be a tendency to create long reading lists without providing the time for attentive reading and re-reading, with the result that the impact of those great books is diminished. Home educators have a great advantage here. If they hold their nerve and are not seduced into thinking that they have to replicate what school does, they can allow their children the time and space they need to read properly—that is, slowly. They can give their children the time and space to re-read.

---

[13] Fr Gabriel Everitt, "Talk 3: Let them learn some of the Psalter," Ampleforth Abbey, accessed October 24, 2017. http://www.abbey.ampleforth.org.uk /sacred-triduum/talk-3-let-them-learn-some-of-the-psalter.

[14] See Jean Leclercq, *The Love of Learning and the Desire for God* (New York: Fordham University Press, 2016) for the roots of this tradition, and Patrick Barry, *A Cloister in the World* (St Louis, MO: Outskirts Press, 2005) for an account of the remarkable Chilean Manquehue movement, which is partly responsible for the revival of *Lectio Divina* in English schools.

The joys of re-reading

Rereading is beneficial because it develops the memory and, hence, the understanding. This was brought home to me recently when we visited a Spitfire museum at one of the Battle of Britain airfields. While we were there, one of our daughters chose to buy a World War II recipe book. It would not have been my first choice of reading, but I am gradually learning to allow her to follow her own interests and enthusiasms, so the book came home and went onto the kitchen shelf. The next day, as we were looking for recipes, we came across all sorts of unappetizing options from the 1940s, ranging from Tripe and Onions to Prune Pudding. As we chatted about various options for supper, I mentioned a dish I was sure she would know nothing about. "Oh yes," she replied. "I've read about it in Laura Ingalls Wilder's books." Hours of reading and rereading about Little Houses in Big Woods, on Prairies and elsewhere had reaped some unexpected dividends.

Fr Gabriel Everitt points out that "Memorization means that meditation often takes very digressive paths, which introduces whole new themes in a way most confusing to logical order. This exuberant approach often takes medieval sermons (those of Augustine, also those of Bernard on the Song of Songs for example) in very varied directions and winding paths."[15] In our house, the winding path led not from St Augustine to St Bernard, but from Spitfires to 19th-century American frontier literature.

What about children who are not educated at home? We need to work especially hard to give them a chance to read and reread, which is very difficult during term time. One of the strengths of slow education is that it helps us rethink the school year. Most schools have a boom and bust approach to education. Teaching is compressed into relatively short chunks, which means that teachers and students get run down toward the end of term and then become ill and collapse in a heap when holidays start. This is a terrible situation, but we tolerate it because we still have long summer holidays, and summer holidays were made for reading.

---

[15] Everitt, "Talk 3: Let them learn some of the Psalter."

In fact, they were made for slow reading, for reading without the pressure of a looming deadline.

But even summer holidays can be misunderstood. What our students need after the busyness of a long term is not a break from work, but true leisure, leisure as understood in the ancient world. As Josef Pieper reminds us: "leisure in Greek is *skole*, and in Latin *scola*, the English 'school.' The word used to designate the place where we educate and teach is derived from a word which means 'leisure.' 'School' does not, properly speaking, mean school, but leisure."[16] Slow education draws on this perception. We do not, or should not, live to work, and leisure is much more than a recharging of the batteries so that we can work. According to the ancients, leisure was the time for true education. That's why so many of Plato's dialogues took place at dinner parties. Leisure, according to Pieper, "is a mental and spiritual attitude—it is not simply the result of external factors, it is not the inevitable result of spare time, a holiday, a weekend or a vacation. . . . Compared with the exclusive ideal of work as activity, leisure implies (in the first place) an attitude of non-activity, of inward calm, of silence; it means not being 'busy,' but letting things happen."[17]

If leisure creates the inner calm that is required for true education, then summer holidays should not be seen as a break from work, but as the time when the best work happens. We should not be compelling our students to do yet more courses and exams in the holidays, but we certainly can encourage them to develop an attitude of non-activity that can then provide the opportunity for reading and rereading, for *intellectus* as well as for *ratio*, for an openness to the reality of things. And that, in the end, is what slow education is all about.

[16] Pieper, *Leisure, the Basis of Culture*, 19–20.
[17] Ibid., 46.

11

Silence

IN HIS WONDERFUL BOOK *The Power of Silence*, Robert Cardinal Sarah argues that silence and attention are closely related: "The silence of listening is a form of attention, a gift of self to the other, and a mark of moral generosity."[1] Silence is therefore a great deal more than simply keeping quiet: it is the means by which communion becomes possible, it is the space in which we can pay attention both to God and other people. "In order to listen," Cardinal Sarah writes, "it is necessary to keep quiet. I do not mean merely a sort of constraint to be physically silent and not to interrupt what someone else is saying, but rather an interior silence, in other words, a silence that not only is directed toward receiving the other person's words but also reflects a heart overflowing with a humble love, capable of full attention, friendly welcome and voluntary self-denial, and strong with the awareness of our poverty."[2]

Silence is not merely a reaction to a world full of noise, nor is it a Romantic rejection of urbanization and industrialization. It is a natural outflowing of any decision to pay attention to another person. When the other to whom we are paying attention is God, we need to remember that He is not distant; in fact, there is "no place on earth where God is more present than in the human heart."[3] If this is the case, then helping our children develop true interiority must become one of our most important tasks, and silence one of our most important educational tools.

[1] Robert Cardinal Sarah, *The Power of Silence: Against the Dictatorship of Noise*, trans. Michael J. Miller (San Francisco: Ignatius Press, 2017), 81.

[2] Ibid.

[3] Ibid., 23.

Silence in schools

If silence is an essential prerequisite for listening to God and other people, then it is not a luxury that we can live or teach without, nor something we should leave to monks and nuns. Unfortunately, the reality is that schools are often very noisy places. As Cardinal Sarah writes, "Even in the schools, silence has disappeared. And yet how can anyone study in the midst of noise? How can you read in noise? How can you train your intellect in noise? How can you structure your thought and the contours of your interior being in noise? How can you be open to the mystery of God, to spiritual values, and to our human greatness in continual turmoil?"[4]

It is easy to justify this continual noise—what do you expect when hundreds of children are in one place?—but we need to ask ourselves what we lose if we don't allow silence to permeate our schools. Matthew Crawford suggests that "The benefits of silence are off the books. They are not measured directly by any econometric instrument such as gross domestic product, yet the availability of silence surely contributes to creativity and innovation. They do not show up explicitly in social statistics such as level of educational achievement, yet one consumes a great deal of silence in the course of becoming educated."[5] "Consume" may not be the most apt verb, but his point is surely a sound one. Where scientism and the cult of the measurable reigns, silence will always suffer.

The progress of monks, Cardinal Sarah reminds us, is also "impossible to measure as it advances."[6] That is because silence is the doorway to a relationship, not a resource to be exploited or squandered. "The shadow of silence allows a man to fix his attention on God,"[7] and neither the relationship itself nor the silence that provides the space in which that relationship develops can be

---

[4] Ibid., 56–57. For a different approach to the same topic see Diana Senechal, *Republic of Noise* (Plymouth, UK: Rowman & Littlefield, 2014) and Helen E. Lees, *Silence in Schools* (London: Institute of Education Press, 2012).

[5] Crawford, *The World Beyond Your Head*, 11.

[6] Sarah, *The Power of Silence*, 73.

[7] Ibid., 74.

measured. Silence is essential, but if we are compelled to justify all our educational decisions with the logic of scientism, we will struggle to convince others of its importance.

However, some might argue that all this misses the point: we all know the importance of silence, but the reason it has largely disappeared from schools is because promoting it would simply be impractical. Home educators might point out that this is a good argument against compulsory schooling rather than an argument against silence, but, even so, it is an objection we need to meet head-on.

Starting with ourselves

So how might we introduce silence into the school and home?

The best place to start is with ourselves. As teachers we often feel the need to perform, which can mean filling in the silences whenever they appear. Cardinal Sarah quotes Henri Nouwen's comment that for ministers the "greatest temptation is toward too many words,"[8] and much the same could be said of teachers. Sometimes we need to keep quiet ourselves so that we can give permission for our students to remain silent as well. Of course, that means that we have to accept that keeping quiet is a genuine and powerful option. I used to write on school reports that students should contribute more actively to lessons and ask more questions to improve their understanding. But, as Evelyn Waugh was quite right to point out in another context, there is a great deal more to active participation than noise: "One participates in a work of art," he pointed out, "when one studies it with reverence and understanding."[9]

If we accept St Thomas's understanding of the ways in which students learn, we have also to accept that teaching does not require a constant stream of words from the teacher. What is more, if we accept that active participation in the liturgy does not require us to indulge in constant chatter, we should also accept

[8] Ibid., 77.

[9] Evelyn Waugh, *The Diaries of Evelyn Waugh*, ed. Michael Davie (London: Penguin, 1979), 793.

that active participation in a lesson does not rely on students talking all the time. If we insist that students should speak at least once in each lesson, we need to ask ourselves if that requirement is for our benefit or theirs. Are we simply attempting to prove that our teaching has made a difference, that learning has taken place, or are we genuinely convinced that learning cannot take place without speech? If that really is the case, are we prepared to follow through on our beliefs and discourage reading? Are we prepared to close our libraries or replace them with "learning resource centers" which are built around collaborative work spaces, banks of computers, and audio resources? Sadly, in many schools, the answer to those questions is Yes. If we want to transform Catholic education, we have to stand out against the trend.

In the end, our approach to silence comes down to what we value. If we value silence in our own lives, we will promote it in our classes. If we allow silence to permeate our homes (without attempting to turn them into Trappist monasteries), we will find that our children become more reflective and more attuned to their interior lives.

Buildings and liturgies

Here are some essential questions for any Catholic school or college:

Are our buildings designed to enhance silence, or are they designed as though noise were the norm? Before I started my teacher training, I spent some time in a little primary school on the outskirts of the English Lake District. The school had been recently rebuilt, nestled in an idyllic setting in one of the loveliest parts of the country. Unfortunately that idyll did not extend to the classrooms themselves, which were open-plan for no sound educational reason that I could fathom. It was hard enough for me as an adult to concentrate on what any of the teachers were saying because noises from one classroom were constantly superimposed on the activities of the next one. Like T.S. Eliot, I was distracted from distraction by distraction. What it was like for children who were still learning to read and write, I can barely imagine.

But we don't need to go as far as open-plan schools to ask questions about sound design. As one of the contributors to the documentary *In Pursuit of Silence* informs us, architects typically spend only a day learning about acoustics during their years of training.[10] It is only the enlightened who give full consideration to the acoustic qualities of their buildings and only the very enlightened who realize that silence is a quality that educational institutions may value.

Do we allow silence to permeate our liturgies? If, to use Cardinal Sarah's pregnant phrase, God does not speak but his voice is clear, we should be quite happy to listen in silence rather than assume that the way to God is to be found through an imitation of popular entertainment. A related question is whether we provide opportunities for Eucharistic Adoration. If Adoration is new to students and staff, we are unlikely to be overwhelmed by crowds of silence-seekers, but that should not stop us from trying. As Cardinal Sarah points out: "developing a taste for prayer is probably the first and foremost battle of our age."[11]

A third question concerns the public events that every school holds so dear: speech days, prize days, sports days, and so on. Do we fill these events with noise? Do we feel obliged to introduce pounding music to create a festive atmosphere, or are we prepared to hold our silent ground? There is a pressing need to be counter-cultural here. In an era where ambient music has become *de rigeur* in shops and public venues, in an age where students shut themselves off from others by plugging in their headphones, the default position is to fill any moment of silence with sound, music, anything. School sports events used to focus on sport: in some schools I have taught in, putting on a pair of trainers is an excuse to pump up the music.

The purpose of silence, it is worth emphasizing again, is not the removal of noise, but the enabling of encounter. In silence we are able to encounter other people and God, which means that we cannot impose silence on our children or students. Silence is not a punishment, nor is it simply a temporary escape so that we

[10] *In Pursuit of Silence*: see http://www.pursuitofsilence.com.
[11] Sarah, *The Power of Silence*, 57.

can regroup before the next verbal onslaught. Silence is part of a wider project that focuses on creating a truly human, truly humane education.

Hesychia

Looking at the Eastern Christian tradition can help us in this regard. In their introduction to *The Philokalia*, G.E.H. Palmer, Philip Sherrard, and Kallistos Ware draw our attention to the word *hesychia*, "a word which not only bears the sense of tranquility and silence (hence our translation: stillness) but also is linked through its Greek root with the idea of being seated, fixed, and so of being concentrated."[12]

This is the type of silence we want in our schools, colleges and home. We want our children to be rooted. We want them to be tranquil. We want them to be comfortable with silence, rather than to be silent all, or even most of, the time. One of our difficulties is that we often see silence and fun as being polar opposites, believing that children can only be silent if they are suppressed or repressed. But that simply isn't true. There is a wonderful moment in *Into Great Silence*, a documentary about the monks of the Grande Chartreuse, when the monks, who (like the film itself) are silent most of the time, go sledging in the Alps.[13] Their pleasure is clear, and their joy is infectious. These are men who know how to be silent, but who also know how to appreciate the simple pleasures in a childlike way. It is sad that so many children cannot.

It is not only our conceptions of monastic silence that get in the way of promoting silence in schools. Another reason we live such noisy lives is because we have become habituated to noise. I took my car into the local garage this week because I was having problems with a headlight. An hour and a lot of headscratching later, I got my car back, with the headlight still not working. As I drove home I went to switch on the radio, only to discover that it

[12] G.E.H. Palmer, Philip Sherrard, Kallistos Ware, *The Philokalia* (New York: Farrar, Straus and Giroux, 1983), 14.

[13] *Into Great Silence*: see www.diegrossestille.de/english.

was now not working either. What was I going to do without either a working radio or, as it turned out, a functioning CD player? How would I be able to bear long journeys? Of course, what I discovered, after I had got over my initial twitchiness, was that the absence of noise was quite liberating. I could remain silent. I could pray for the all the people for whom I had been meaning to pray. I could practice the presence of God.

This is what silence is all about. It is living in the here and now, being open to God and to other people, being available to others. How could we possibly manage without it?

12

Work and
the Work of Schools

ABOUT FIFTY YEARS AGO, a parishioner at our church published a book about good work. In this book, the author asked:

> What can be the meaning of "education" or of "good work" when nothing counts except that which can be precisely stated, measured, counted, or weighed? Neither mathematics nor geometry, neither physics nor chemistry can entertain qualitative notions like good or bad, higher or lower. They can entertain only quantitative notions of more or less. It is easy, therefore, to distinguish between less education and more education, and between less work and more work, but a qualitative evaluation of education or of work...? How could that be possible?[1]

With that simple but profound paragraph about education and work, E. F. Schumacher stirred up a lot of trouble. If one of the leading economists of his day was prepared to ask questions like these, the status quo became difficult to justify. If work wasn't the issue, but good work was, then maybe, just maybe, mainstream thinking about education and the world of work needed to be reappraised.

The purpose of work

Work is not a topic that often sets the heart racing, but maybe that is because our conception of work has become impover-

---

[1] Schumacher, *Good Work*, 112–13.

ished. If work is simply what brings in an income, if our everyday experience is that we have either too much or too little work, we are hardly going to want to think any more about it. If work is simply an obligation we have to fulfill in order to survive, it makes sense for us to dream about our next holiday, to have the Monday morning blues, and to hang on desperately until we retire and get the whole experience out of our system. Perhaps, however, Schumacher was right. Maybe we should be doing a great deal more than simply helping our children into a career. Maybe we should be teaching them about good work and showing them what it means in practice.

As Catholics, we know that work has great value. Made in the image of God, we are "sub-creators," to use Tolkien's phrase: "We make still by the law in which we're made."[2] That is why we cannot accept utilitarian conceptions of work. That is why, like Schumacher, we have to return to the most fundamental questions if we are to make sense of work, including the work of schools. Specifically, we have to return to two questions we have already encountered in this book: what is the purpose of education? and why do we value only what can be measured or counted?

Schumacher was quite clear that unless we have a sense of what work is for, we will never be able to distinguish good work from bad:

> As long as we persist in our arrogance, which dismisses the entirety of traditional wisdom as "pre-scientific" and therefore not to be taken seriously, fit only for the museum, there is no basis for any education other than training for worldly success. Education for good work is quite impossible; how could we possibly distinguish good work from bad work if human life on earth has no meaning or purpose? The word "good" presupposes an aim: good for what? Good for making money; good for promotion; good for fame or power? All this may be

[2] J.R.R. Tolkien, "Mythopoeia," in *Tree and Leaf* (London: Unwin Hyman, 1991), 99.

attained by work which, from another point of view, would be considered very bad work.[3]

Good work is now back on the political agenda. The British government recently commissioned a report into the issue, which resulted in 116 pages.[4] This report makes interesting reading, but what is striking about it is what it misses—the purpose, or end, of work is scarcely mentioned. If we don't examine the purpose of work, we can easily find ourselves stuck in a dispiriting cul-de-sac. If we don't interrogate the end of work, the education we offer our children is likely to go off-kilter.

Pieper and Newman on work

Of course, Schumacher is not the only Catholic thinker to have drawn our attention to notions of good work. In his most famous book, *Leisure, the Basis of Culture*, Josef Pieper attempted to demolish the ideal of total work and to recover a more authentic understanding of work from a Christian perspective. Blessed John Henry Newman also challenged worldly conceptions of work and success, famously saying that

> God has created me to do Him some definite service; He has committed some work to me which He has not committed to another. I have my mission—I never may know it in this life, but I shall be told it in the next. Somehow I am necessary for His purposes, as necessary in my place as an Archangel in his—if, indeed, I fail, He can raise another, as He could make the stones children of Abraham. Yet I have a part in this great work; I am a link in a chain, a bond of connexion between persons. He has not created me for naught. I shall do good, I shall do His work; I shall be an angel of peace, a preacher of truth in

---

[3] Schumacher, *Good Work*, 114.

[4] Matthew Taylor, "Good Work: the Taylor Review of Modern Working Practices," Department for Business, Energy & Industrial Strategy, accessed October 26, 2017. https://www.gov.uk/government/publications/good-work-the-taylor-review-of-modern-working-practices.

my own place, while not intending it, if I do but keep His commandments and serve Him in my calling.

Therefore I will trust Him. Whatever, wherever I am, I can never be thrown away. If I am in sickness, my sickness may serve Him; in perplexity, my perplexity may serve Him; if I am in sorrow, my sorrow may serve Him. My sickness, or perplexity, or sorrow may be necessary causes of some great end, which is quite beyond us. He does nothing in vain; He may prolong my life, He may shorten it; He knows what He is about. He may take away my friends, He may throw me among strangers, He may make me feel desolate, make my spirits sink, hide the future from me—still He knows what He is about.[5]

All of which pulls the rug out from under the usual conceptions of success by which schools are measured or by which they measure themselves.

MacIntyre in conversation

Alasdair MacIntyre has deconstructed dominant attitudes toward work in other ways. In a conversation with Joseph Dunne, he pointed out that "what the current system requires of teachers is the production of the kind of compliant manpower that the current economy needs, with the different levels of skill and kinds of skill that are required in a hierarchically ordered economy." But the production of "compliant manpower" should never be the aim of any Catholic institution. According to MacIntyre, "what education has to aim at for each and every child if it is not to be a mockery, is both the development of those powers that enable children to become reflective and independent members of their families and political communities and the inculcation of those

---

[5] John Henry Newman, "Meditations on Christian Doctrine," Newman Reader, accessed October 25, 2017, http://www.newmanreader.org/works/meditations/meditations9.html.

virtues that are needed to direct us towards the achievement of our common and individual goods."[6]

This is a noble and inspiring vision of work, but the only problem is that noble and inspiring visions tend to clash with contemporary realities. MacIntyre's own assessment is, therefore, very bleak: "insofar as such education is successful," he writes, "it will to a remarkable extent render those who profit from it unfit to participate compliantly and successfully in the social and economic order. For they will have learned how to ask questions about the activities presented by that order which it is important—from the standpoint of that order—not to ask."

I am not convinced that we have to go quite that far, but it is certainly true that asking questions about the purpose of education and the nature of good work will upset many people in educational authority, whether Catholic or not. However, we cannot let go of the idea that Catholic education should be built on a fully human ecology. If our conceptions of work are too narrow, humans will never be fulfilled, and if our conceptions of what it is to be human are too narrow, work will struggle to become good. As Pope Benedict XVI wrote in *Caritas in Veritate*, "authentic human development concerns the whole of the person in every single dimension. Without the perspective of human life, human progress in this world is denied breathing space. Enclosed within history, it runs the risk of being reduced to the mere accumulation of wealth."[7] And as Blessed Paul VI wrote in *Populorum Progressio*, integral human development promotes the fulfillment "of every man and of the whole man."[8]

As Catholic educators, therefore, we have to ask ourselves two key questions: firstly, is the education we are providing our children, whether at home or at school or college, built upon these

[6] Alasdair MacIntyre and Joseph Dunne, "Alasdair MacIntyre on Education: In Dialogue with Joseph Dunne," *Journal of Philosophy of Education*, 36, no.1 (2002): 1–19, doi:10.1111/1467-9752.00256.

[7] Benedict XVI, *Caritas in Veritate*, 11.

[8] Paul VI, *Populorum Progressio*, 42, Vatican website, accessed October 25, 2017, http://w2.vatican.va/content/paul-vi/en/encyclicals/documents/hf_p-vi_enc_26031967_populorum.html.

solid principles? Secondly, are we preparing students, both implicitly and explicitly, for good work? Too often, we provide an unbalanced education for our children. We focus on certain aspects of human development rather than others. Maybe we emphasize the life of the mind at the expense of the work of the hands. Maybe we focus on exam success rather than on the development of wisdom. Maybe we consider the curriculum and neglect the poor at our gates. The imbalance will vary from place to place, but what is clear is that a Catholic education must, by its very nature, be a complete education. It must resist fragmentation and it must work for the good of the whole man and all men.

Work and education in Great Expectations

All of which brings me back to Charles Dickens. As a child, I passed Restoration House, the model for Satis House in *Great Expectations*, every day on the way to school. When I walked up the High Street I passed the Bull Hotel, which was the inspiration for the Blue Boar. If we wanted a good meal out, we went to a restaurant which was the site of Pumblechook's seed shop. The world of *Great Expectations* was our world. Ours too was the marsh country, down by the river. But it was only many years later, when I took English as a degree, that I actually read the book. It soon became not just my favorite Dickens novel but one of my favorite novels by any author. [9]

Great Expectations is a novel about class, pride, and crime. It is a book about the city and the countryside, about England and empire. It deals with love and death, hope and revenge, failure and success. But it is also a novel about work and education. We might recall, for instance, the relationship between Pip and Joe Gargery. Though Pip works for Joe, their relationship is grounded in something greater than work. Joe loves Pip and is his greatest protector, though Pip soon rejects his teaching and what he sees as the constraints of the blacksmith's life because he

---

[9] Charles Dickens, *Great Expectations* (Oxford: Oxford University Press, 1994).

is deceived by Miss Havisham, whose response to personal rejection is a life of exploitative relationships. Miss Havisham is aided and abetted by Mr Pumblechook, whose work, emblematically, consists of selling seeds (or pips) that are shut away from the light to prevent them from growing and whose idea of education is to demean Pip and to fire sums at him wherever he has the opportunity. Between them, Miss Havisham and Mr Pumblechook offer a model of education that is severely limited and that leads only to frustration and pain.

It is against this backdrop that we should read Joe's attempts to save Pip further pain at home and at work. What Joe tries to give Pip is a good home, a good education and good work. In these attempts he is frustrated first by his wife, Pip's sister, and then by Pip himself, who soon wants nothing more than to escape home, work and education in order to fulfill his great expectations. We also need to add Biddy, Pip's friend and "first teacher," into this complex situation. Biddy's teaching career begins unpromisingly in the school where she is a pupil and where the supposed teacher, Mr Wopsle's great aunt, spends most of her time in "a state of coma." As a consequence, the pupils enter "upon a competitive examination on the subject of Boots, with the view of ascertaining who could tread the hardest upon whose toes."

> This mental exercise lasted until Biddy made a rush at them and distributed three defaced Bibles (shaped as if they had been unskillfully cut off the chump-end of something), more illegibly printed at the best than any curiosities of literature I have since met with, speckled all over with ironmould, and having various specimens of the insect world smashed between their leaves. This part of the Course was usually lightened by several single combats between Biddy and refractory students. When the fights were over, Biddy gave out the number of a page, and then we all read aloud what we could—or what we couldn't—in a frightful chorus; Biddy leading with a high shrill monotonous voice, and none of us having the least notion of, or reverence for, what we were reading about. When this horrible din had lasted a cer-

tain time, it mechanically awoke Mr. Wopsle's great-aunt, who staggered at a boy fortuitously, and pulled his ears.[10]

Despite this hugely unpromising start, Biddy eventually resolves to become a schoolmistress and to provide a higher standard of education than was ever provided by Mr Wopsle's great-aunt. The way she explains her plan to Pip is hugely revealing: "I can be well recommended by all the neighbors, and I hope I can be industrious and patient, and teach myself while I teach others."[11] Like Joe, Biddy is a true craftsman: she knows that she has to learn herself in order to teach; she also knows that her task requires time and patience; and, furthermore, she understands, as do the neighbors who recommend her, the importance of character. What is more, she knows what she doesn't need: she doesn't speak about becoming an expert in her field or buying the latest technology. She knows that what she is able to give her students is herself.

The marriage of Biddy and Joe toward the end of the book is therefore much more than a romantic triumph. It also brings together two models of education and two models of work into one perfect combination, into one loving home. Joe is no academic and Biddy is no blacksmith, but between them they are able to offer their students, their apprentices and, we are led to believe, their children the sort of education Pip was never able to have himself. While Joe continues to work primarily with his hands and Biddy primarily with her head, the two of them refuse to accept any form of Cartesian dualism. Neither looks down on the other's work: together they are great spouses and parents. Dickens was not idealistic, but he did have ideals, and, in Joe and Biddy, he provided an image of an ideal family, an ideal education, and an ideal of good work. If only I had known that when I was wandering around Rochester dressed as a chimney sweep.

---

[10] Dickens, *Great Expectations*, 72.
[11] Ibid., 279.

Utilitarian conceptions of work

This foray into the world of imaginative literature might seem like an indulgence in a chapter about work, but I would argue that Catholic education can sometimes suffer from a crisis of narrative. What it needs is not just stories but good stories, just as students need good work and not just work. That is why E. F. Schumacher refused to confine his discussion to practicalities— to what he had learned while working at the National Coal Board or as an advisor for governments around the world. Just as there is more to education than instruction, so, he believed, there is more to work than jobs. That is one reason why he insisted that education for good work should begin with metaphysics. "If we continue to teach that the human being is *nothing but* the outcome of a mindless, meaningless, and purposeless process of evolution, a process of 'selection' for survival, that is to say, the outcome of nothing but *utilitarianism*—we only come to a *utilitarian* idea of work: that work is *nothing but* a more or less unpleasant necessity, and the less there is of it the better."[12]

It is very easy for Catholic educators to slip into utilitarian ways of thinking. It is easy to work with life-limiting narratives, to base our approach on limited stories we have unwittingly internalized. We may provide an excellent Catholic education, but when it comes to providing career advice, we slip into secular ways of thinking: the whole point of education, we imply, is going to college and starting a career. It doesn't much matter what career, as long as it pays well. Schumacher knew that such an approach was not good enough. He worked with a different narrative and with a different set of presuppositions. "Maybe higher education," he wrote,

> could be designed to lead to a *different* world of work— different from the one we have today. This, indeed, would be my most sincere hope. But how could this be as long as higher education clings to the metaphysics of materialistic scientism and its doctrine of mindless evolution? It cannot be. Figs cannot grow on thistles. Good work can-

[12] Schumacher, *Good Work*, 121.

not grow out of such metaphysics. To try to make it grow from such a base can do nothing but increase the prevailing confusion. The most urgent need of our time is and remains the need for *metaphysical reconstruction*, a supreme effort to bring clarity into our deepest convictions with regard to the questions: What is man? Where does he come from? and What is the purpose of his life?[13]

Which brings us full circle. Like Pip, we have returned to where we started. The question that now confronts us is *where do we go next?*

---

[13] Ibid., 123.

PART FOUR

Reflection

Conclusion
Transforming Catholic Education

CHOOSING *How to Transform Catholic Education* as a subtitle was always a risky decision. On the few occasions I have mentioned it in conversation, the obvious question has been fired back at me: How do you? The answer is that there is no formula. There are no rules that need to be followed.

This is not simply a copout. Education is not a children's dot-to-dot puzzle. Education is meant for people, and people cannot be reduced to formulae, rules, or dots on a page. That is why scientism doesn't work—and if a reductionist approach doesn't work for humans, how much less will it work for God?

Nonetheless, a conclusion is a conclusion, and so I will endeavor to at least pull a few threads together. Throughout this book, I have worked with the assumption that getting the foundations right will give us the chance to transform Catholic education. If our essential ideas are confused or just plain wrong, we will quickly lose our way. If our presuppositions are not fully Catholic, we will soon succumb to the secular forces that surround us. That is why I addressed issues like parenting and presentism, and why I challenged consumerism, relativism, and scientism.

However, Catholic education will not be transformed by theory alone. That is why I have written about slow education and the importance of silence. That is why I have sprinkled practical suggestions throughout the book—though I am acutely aware that these practical suggestions must be applied to individual families, schools and colleges, all of which are different, all of which face their own unique challenges. The transformation of Catholic education is a task for us all—or, more accurately, the transformation of Catholic education is God's work, and we all need to ask him what our particular contributions could be.

Parents and transformation

I wrote in Chapter 1 that, for Catholic education to be transformed, we need to recognize that parents are their children's
primary educators and to act upon that recognition. Catholic
education will not be transformed by the Pope, by governments,
by school boards or by bishops' conferences, though each of
these has a valuable role. It will not even be transformed by headteachers, crucial though their job is. Nor should teachers believe
that they have the power to effect transformation in our time.

If Catholic education is to be transformed, families must be the
vanguard. Whether they educate their children at home or send
them to school, whether they are homeschoolers or unschoolers,
whether they operate within the state system or not, parents are
the ones who will create the transformation we need.

There is a lot of talk at the moment about personalized education. This is what parents offer and have always offered. Human
scale education is another fascinating educational movement, but
the most human scale education of all is to be found in the family.
There is a desire in many places for what are known as Relational
Schools, but there is no relationship more essential and long-last-
ing than that between parents and their children—at least, no
relationship on earth. If Catholic education is to be transformed,
it is families who will do it.

But families face a huge number of challenges. The task of
transforming Catholic education may well seem like a job too far
for parents who are struggling to pay the bills, to manage the
house, and to raise their children in the Faith. This is why we
need to put supporting families at the top of our agenda. Our
first priority is not looking after buildings, building schools, or
recruiting teachers. Our first priority is to support our families.
That is why the parish is so important. That is why mutual support groups matter. That is why small is still beautiful.

What to do

If pressed for a soundbite, I would answer as follows: parents are
the primary educators. Take that idea seriously, and transforma-

tion will happen. But I would rather not resort to soundbites, so, for the final word, I will return to E. F. Schumacher, quoting a passage from *Good Work* and changing just one word. He wrote about industry, but it seems to me that what he wrote could equally well apply to education. If we want to know what to do next, this is as good an answer as any:

> The greatest "doing" that is open to every one of us, now as always, is to foster and develop within oneself a genuine understanding of the situation which confronts us, and to build conviction, determination, and persuasiveness upon such understanding. Let us face it, to look at modern [education] in the light of the Gospels is not the fashion of the day, and the diagnosis I have given here is not acceptable, at this point in time, to the great majority of our contemporaries. What, then, is the use of asking for a "programme of action"? Those who have understood know what to do. They also know that, although in a minority, they do not stand alone.[1]

---

[1] Schumacher, *Good Work*, 37–38.

Bibliography

Anderson, Carl and José Granados. *Called to Love: Approaching John Paul II's Theology of the Body.* New York: Random House, 2009.

Andres, Suzie. *A Little Way of Homeschooling: Thirteen Families Discover Catholic Unschooling.* Lake Ariel, PA: Hillside Education, 2011.

———. *Homeschooling with Gentleness.* Lake Ariel, PA: Hillside Education, 2015.

St Athanasius on the Incarnation. Cambridge: Cambridge University Press, 1989.

Auden, W.H. "New Year Letter." In *Collected Longer Poems*, 77–130. London: Faber and Faber, 1968.

Barr, Stephen M. *Science and Religion: The Myth of Conflict.* London: Catholic Truth Society, 2011.

Barry, Patrick. *A Cloister in the World.* St Louis, MO: Outskirts Press, 2005.

Caldecott, Stratford. *Beauty for Truth's Sake: On the Re-enchantment of Education.* Grand Rapids, MI: Brazos Press, 2009.

———. *Beauty in the Word: Rethinking the Foundations of Education.* Tacoma, WA: Angelico Press, 2012.

Calhoun, Craig J., Mark Juergensmeyer, and Jonathan VanAntwerpen. *Rethinking Secularism.* New York: Oxford University Press, 2011.

Carr, Nicholas. *The Shallows: How the Internet is Changing the Way We Think, Read and Remember.* London: Atlantic Books, 2010.

Cavalletti, Sofia, Patricia Coulter, Gianna Gobi, and Silvana Q. Montanaro. *The Good Shepherd & The Child: A Joyful Journey.* Chicago, IL: Liturgy Training Publications, 1994.

Chesterton, G.K. *What's Wrong with the World*, in *The Collected Works of G.K. Chesterton*, vol. IV. San Francisco: Ignatius Press, 1987.

Christodoulou, Daisy. *Seven Myths about Education.* London: Routledge, 2014.

Claxton, Guy. *Intelligence in the Flesh.* London: Yale University Press, 2015.

Community of Franciscan Sisters of the Renewal Newsletter, Fall 2017.

Crawford, Matthew B. *The World Beyond Your Head: On Becoming an Individual in an Age of Distraction*. London: Penguin, 2016.

Csikszentmihalyi, Mihaly. *Flow and the Foundations of Positive Psychology: The Collected Works of Mihaly Csikszentmihalyi*. Berlin: Springer, 2014.

Culpin, Chris, Dale Danham, Ian Dawson, and Maggie Wilson. *SHP History: Year 7, Pupil's Book*. London: Hodder Education, 2008.

Dickens, Charles. *A Tale of Two Cities*. Ware: Wordsworth Editions, 1999.

———. *Great Expectations*. Oxford: Oxford University Press, 1994.

Dolan, Paul. *Happiness by Design: Finding Pleasure and Purpose in Everyday Life*. London: Penguin, 2015.

Duffy, Eamon. *The Voices of Morebath: Reformation and Rebellion in an English Village*. New Haven: Yale University Press, 2001.

Eagleton, Terry. *Materialism*. New Haven: Yale University Press, 2016.

Fitzgerald, F. Scott. *The Great Gatsby*. Oxford: Oxford University Press, 1998.

Garton Ash, Timothy. *History of the Present: Essays, Sketches, and Dispatches from Europe in the 1900s*. New York: Vintage Books, 2001.

Gatto, John Taylor. *Dumbing Us Down: The Hidden Curriculum of Compulsory Schooling*. Gabriola Island, BC: New Society Publishers, 2017.

Gelernter, David. *The Tides of Mind: Uncovering the Spectrum of Consciousness*. New York: W. W. Norton, 2016.

Goldacre, Ben. *Bad Science*. London: Harper Perennial, 2009.

Gratton, Lynda. *The Shift: The Future of Work is Already Here*. London: William Collins, 2014.

Guardini, Romano. *Letters from Lake Como*. Translated by Geoffrey W. Bromiley. Grand Rapids, MI: W.B. Eerdmans, 1994.

Guldi, Jo, and David Armitage. *The History Manifesto*. Cambridge: Cambridge University Press, 2014.

Hannoum, Abdelmajid. "What is an Order of Time?" *History and Theory*, 47: 458–71. doi:10.1111/j.1468-2303.2008.00468.x.

Hartog, François. *Croire en l'histoire*. Paris: Flammarion, 2013.

———. *Regimes of Historicity: Presentism and Experiences of Time*. Translated by Saskia Brown. New York: Columbia University Press, 2015.

Heath, Sr Dominic Mary. "Giving God Our Attention: Learning the Virtue of Studiousness." *Plough Quarterly*, Summer 2017.

Hirsch, E.D. *Why Knowledge Matters: Rescuing our Children from Failed Educational Theories*. Cambridge, MA: Harvard Education Press, 2016.

Hodgson, Peter E. *Theology and Modern Physics*. Aldershot: Ashgate, 2005.

Holt, John. *How Children Learn*. London: Penguin, 1991.

Huffington, Arianna. *Thrive: The Third Metric to Redefining Success and Creating a Life of Well-being, Wisdom, and Wonder*. London: Random House, 2014.

John Paul II. *Man and Woman He Created Them: A Theology of the Body*. Translated by Michael Waldstein. Boston, MA: Pauline Books and Media, 2006.

Kelly, Kathleen and Sylvia Phillips. *Teaching Literacy to Learners with Dyslexia: A Multi-sensory Approach*. London: Sage, 2011.

Krznaric, Roman. *Carpe Diem Regained: The Vanishing Art of Seizing the Day*. London: Unbound, 2017.

Kubey, Robert. "Television Dependence, Diagnosis, and Prevention: With Commentary on Video Games, Pornography, and Media Education." In *Tuning In To Young Viewers: Social Science Perspectives on Television*, edited by Tannis M. MacBeth. London: Sage, 1996.

Leclercq, Jean. *The Love of Learning and the Desire for God*. New York: Fordham University Press, 2016.

Lees, Helen E. *Silence in Schools*. London: Institute of Education Press, 2012.

Lewis, C.S. *Poetry and Prose in the Sixteenth Century*. Oxford: Clarendon Press, 1997.

———. *The Screwtape Letters: Letters from a Senior to a Junior Devil*. London: Macmillan, 1961.

Lipovetsky, Gilles. *Hypermodern Times*. Translated by Andrew Brown. Cambridge: Polity, 2005.

Louv, Richard. *Last Child in the Woods*. North Carolina: Algonquin Books of Chapel Hill, 2006.

Macdonald, Helen. *H is for Hawk*. London: Vintage Classic, 2016.

MacIntyre, Alasdair and Joseph Dunne. "Alasdair MacIntyre on Education: In Dialogue with Joseph Dunne." *Journal of Philosophy of Education*, 36, no.1 (2002): 1–19. doi:10.1111/1467-9752.00256.

Maffei, Lamberto. *Hâte-toi lentement: sommes-nous programmés pour la vitesse du monde numérique?* Translated by Lucia Di Bisceglie with Camille Zabka. Limoges: Fyp éditions, 2016.

McLuhan, Marshall. *The Medium Is the Massage: An Inventory of Effects.* Berkeley, CA: Gingko Press, 2013.

———. *Understanding Media.* London: ARK, 1987.

Meier, Christian. *From Athens to Auschwitz: The Uses of History.* Translated by Deborah Lucas Schneider. Cambridge, MA: Harvard University Press, 2005.

Montessori, Maria. *The Discovery of the Child.* Delhi: Aaker Books, 2004.

———. *The Montessori Method.* New York: Frederick A Stokes, 1912.

Newman, John Henry. *The Idea of a University.* Dublin: Publication of the International Centre for Newman Studies, 2005.

O'Connor, Flannery. *Mystery and Manners: Occasional Prose.* New York: Farrar, Straus & Giroux, 1970.

OECD. *The Nature of Learning: Using Research to Inspire Practice.* Paris: OECD, 2011.

Orr, David. *Hope is an Imperative.* Washington, DC: Island Press, 2011.

———. *The Nature of Design.* New York: Oxford University Press, 2002.

Orwell, George. "Pleasure Spots." *Tribune,* January 11, 1946.

Palmer, G.E.H., Philip Sherrard, Kallistos Ware. *The Philokalia.* New York: Farrar, Straus and Giroux, 1983.

Peachey, Roy. "Book Boxes for Schools and Families." *The Universe Education Supplement,* September/October 2017.

Pearson. "Find out about the potential for AI in the Classroom and how Colin could work," undated.

Pennac, Daniel. *School Blues.* London: MacLehose Press, 2010.

Pernoud, Régine. *Those Terrible Middle Ages: Debunking the Myths.* Translated by Anne Englund Nash. San Francisco: Ignatius Press, 2000.

Pieper, Josef. *Happiness and Contemplation.* South Bend, IN: St Augustine's Press, 1998.

———. *Leisure, the Basis of Culture.* San Francisco: Ignatius Press, 2009.

Polkinghorne, John. *Science and Providence: God's Interaction with the World.* Cambridge: International Society for Science and Religion, 2007.

Postman, Neil. *Amusing Ourselves to Death: Public Discourse in the Age of Show Business.* New York: Viking, 1985.

———. *The End of Education: Redefining the Value of School*. New York: Vintage, 1995.

———. *Technopoly: The Surrender of Culture to Technology*. New York: Vintage, 1993.

Riley, Gina & Peter Gray. "Grown Unschoolers' Experiences with Higher Education and Employment: Report II on a Survey of 75 Unschooled Adults." *Other Education: The Journal of Educational Alternatives* Vol. 4, Issue 2 (2015): 33–53.

Robinson, Marilynne. *When I Was a Child I Read Books*. London: Virago, 2013.

Roszak, Theodore. *The Cult of Information: The Folklore of Computers and the True Art of Thinking*. London: Paladin, 1988.

Sacks, Oliver. *Uncle Tungsten: Memories of a Chemical Boyhood*. London: Picador, 2016.

Sarah, Robert. *The Power of Silence: Against the Dictatorship of Noise*. Translated by Michael J. Miller. San Francisco: Ignatius Press, 2017.

Schumacher, E. F. *Good Work*. London: Jonathan Cape, 1979.

———. *Small is Beautiful*. London: Abacus, 1987.

Sebald, W.G. *Austerlitz*. London: Hamish Hamilton, 2001.

Senechal, Diana. *Republic of Noise*. Plymouth, UK: Rowman & Littlefield, 2014.

Shakespeare, William and Roma Gill. *Julius Caesar*. Oxford: Oxford University Press, 2001.

Sigman, Aric. *Remotely Controlled: How Television is Damaging Our Lives*. London: Vermilion, 2005.

———. *The Spoilt Generation: Why Restoring Authority Will Make Our Children and Society Happier*. London: Piatkus, 2009.

———. "Time for a View on Screen Time." *Archives of Disease in Childhood* 97 (2012): 935–42.

Somerville, C. John. *The Decline of the Secular University*. New York: Oxford University Press, 2006.

Spark, Muriel. *The Prime of Miss Jean Brodie*. London: Macmillan, 1961.

Springer, Simon. "Learning Through The Soles of Our Feet: Unschooling, Anarchism, and the Geography of Childhood." In *The Radicalization of Pedagogy*, edited by Simon Springer, Marcelo Lopes de Souza, and Richard J. White, 247–65. London: Rowman & Littlefield, 2016.

Taylor, Charles. *A Secular Age*. Cambridge, MA: Belknap Press of Harvard University Press, 2007.

Tolkien, J.R.R. "Mythopoeia." In *Tree and Leaf*. London: Unwin Hyman, 1991.

Turkle, Sherry. *Alone Together*. New York: Basic Books, 2012.

Urteaga, Jesus. *God and Children*. Manila, Philippines: Sinag-Tala, 1984.

Vodolazkin, Eugene. *Laurus*. Translated by Lisa C. Hayden. London: Oneworld, 2015.

Warner, Michael, Jonathan VanAntwerpen, and Craig Calhoun. *Varieties of Secularism in a Secular Age*. Cambridge, MA: Harvard University Press, 2010.

Waugh, Evelyn. *The Diaries of Evelyn Waugh*. Edited by Michael Davie. London: Penguin, 1979.

Weigel, George. *Witness to Hope: The Biography of Pope John Paul II*. London: HarperCollins, 2001.

Willingham, Daniel T. *Why Don't Students Like School?: A Cognitive Scientist Answers Questions About How the Mind Works and What it Means for the Classroom*. San Francisco, CA: Jossey-Bass, 2009.

Zink, Michel. *Bienvenue au Moyen-Âge*. Paris: Editions des Equateurs / France Inter, 2015.

Websites

42. "Disrupting Engineering Education." Accessed October 24 2017. https://www.42.us.org.

Alves, Julio. "Unintentional Knowledge: What We Find When We're Not Looking." Accessed 24 October 2017. http://www.chronicle.com/article/Unintentional-Knowledge/139891.

Aquinas, St Thomas. *De Veritate*. Accessed October 25, 2017. http://dhspriory.org/thomas/QDdeVer11.htm.

———. *Summa Theologica*. Accessed October 24, 2017, http://dhspriory.org/thomas/summa/FP/FP117.html#FPQ117OUTP1.

Bath Spa University. "An Introduction to Attachment and the Implications for Learning and Behaviour." Accessed October 23, 2017. https://www.bathspa.ac.uk/media/bathspaacuk/education-/research/digital-literacy/education-resource-introduction-to-attachment.pdf.

Benedict XVI. "Address of his Holiness Benedict XVI to the Participants in the International Congress Organized to Commemorate the 40th Anniversary of the Dogmatic Constitution on Divine Revelation 'Dei Verbum.'" Accessed October 24, 2017, http://w2.vatican.va/content/benedict-xvi/en/speeches/2005/september/documents/hf_ben-xvi_spe_20050916_40-dei-verbum.html.

———. "Address of the Holy Father to Pupils." Accessed October 23, 2017. https://w2.vatican.va/content/benedict-xvi/en/speeches/2010/september/documents/hf_ben-xvi_spe_20100917_mondo-educ.html#ADDRESS_OF_THE_HOLY_FATHER_TO_PUPILS.

———. "Address of the Holy Father to Teachers and Religious." Accessed October 24, 2017, https://w2.vatican.va/content/benedict-xvi/en/speeches/2010/september/documents/hf_ben-xvi_spe_20100917_mondo-educ.html#ADDRESS_OF_THE_HOLY_FATHER_TO_TEACHERS_AND_RELIGIOUS.

———. *Caritas in Veritate*. Accessed October 24, 2017. http://w2.vatican.va/content/benedict-xvi/en/encyclicals/documents/hf_ben-xvi_enc_20090629_caritas-in-veritate.html.

———. "Meeting with Catholic Educators." Accessed October 24, 2017. https://w2.vatican.va/content/benedict-xvi/en/speeches/2008/april/documents/hf_ben-xvi_spe_20080417_cath-univ-washington.html.

———. "Meeting with the World of Culture." Accessed October 23, 2017. https://w2.vatican.va/content/benedict-xvi/en/speeches/2010/may/documents/hf_ben-xvi_spe_20100512_incontro-cultura.html.

Bond, Jeffrey. "The Modes of Teaching." Accessed October 24, 2017, https://thejosias.com/2015/04/16/the-modes-of-teaching-part-iii.

Catechism of the Catholic Church. Accessed October 23, 2017. http://www.vatican.va/archive/ccc_css/archive/catechism/p3s2c2a6.htm.

Chesterton, G.K. *Tremendous Trifles*. Accessed October 24, 2017, http://www.gutenberg.org/files/8092/8092-h/8092-h.htm.

Code of Canon Law. Accessed October 23, 2017. http://www.vatican.va/archive/ENG1104/_INDEX.HTM.

Common Sense Media. "The Common Sense Census: Media Use by Tweens and Teens." Accessed October 24, 2017. https://www.commonsensemedia.org/sites/default/files/uploads/research/census_researchreport.pdf.

Crawford, Matthew B. "Science Education and Liberal Education." Accessed October 24, 2017. http://www.thenewatlantis.com/pub

lications/science-education-and-liberal-education.

———. "The Computerized Academy." Accessed October 24, 2017, http://www.thenewatlantis.com/publications/the-computerized-academy.

Egan, Philip. "The Future of Our Catholic Schools." Accessed October 23, 2017. http://www.portsmouthdiocese.org.uk/bishop/pastoral_letters/20161002-BoP-PL-Catholic-Schools-A4.pdf.

———. "The Future of Our Diocesan Schools." Accessed October 23, 2017. http://www.portsmouthdiocese.org.uk/bishop/docs/20151106-BoP-The-Future-of-our-Diocesan-Schools.pdf.

Escriva, Josemaria. "Questions About the Family," Accessed October 24, 2017. http://www.josemariaescriva.info/article/14-questions-about-the-family.

Everitt, Gabriel. "Talk 3: Let them learn some of the Psalter." Accessed October 24, 2017. http://www.abbey.ampleforth.org.uk/sacred-triduum/talk-3-let-them-learn-some-of-the-psalter.

Forest School Association. "Good Practice." Accessed October 24, 2017, http://www.forestschoolassociation.org/full-principles-and-criteria-for-good-practice.

———. "What is Forest School?" Accessed October 24, 2017. http://www.forestschoolassociation.org/what-is-forest-school.

Francis. *Laudato Si'*. Accessed October 24, 2017, http://w2.vatican.va/content/francesco/en/encyclicals/documents/papa-francesco_20150524_enciclica-laudato-si.html.

———. "The Family 3.—The Father." Accessed October 24, 2017, https://w2.vatican.va/content/francesco/en/audiences/2015/documents/papa-francesco_20150128_udienza-generale.html.

———. "The Family—15. Education." Accessed October 23, 2017. https://w2.vatican.va/content/francesco/en/audiences/2015/documents/papa-francesco_20150520_udienza-generale.html.

Gaudium et Spes. Accessed October 24, 2017. http://www.vatican.va/archive/hist_councils/ii_vatican_council/documents/vat-ii_cons_19651207_gaudium-et-spes_en.html.

Gove, Michael. "What Does it Mean to Be an Educated Person." Accessed October 24, 2017, https://www.gov.uk/government/speeches/what-does-it-mean-to-be-an-educated-person.

Gravissimum Educationis. Accessed October 23, 2017. http://www.vatican.va/archive/hist_councils/ii_vatican_council/documents/vat-ii_decl_19651028_gravissimum-educationis_en.html.

Hadjadj, Fabrice. "Rediscovering the 'Language of Wood': Why Can't We Just Substitute 'Be Fruitful and Multiply' with 'Connect and Download'?" Accessed October 24, 2017, http://humanumreview.com/articles/rediscovering-the-language-of-wood-why-cant-we-just-substitute-be-fruitful-and-multiply-with-connect-and-download.

Halls, Andrew. "Why We're Weaning Pupils Off Literary Fast Food." Accessed October 24, 2017, https://www.kcs.org.uk/media/1062/2017_03_26-why-were-weaning-pupils-off-literary-fast-food.pdf.

Hirsch, E. D. "You Can Always Look It Up—Or Can You?" Accessed October 24, 2017, http://special.edschool.virginia.edu/papers/hirsch_liu.html.

Into Great Silence. Accessed October 24, 2017. www.diegrossestille.de/english.

In Pursuit of Silence. Accessed October 24, 2017. http://www.pursuitofsilence.com.

John Paul II. *Fides et Ratio.* Accessed October 24, 2017. https://w2.vatican.va/content/john-paul-ii/en/encyclicals/documents/hf_jp-ii_enc_14091998_fides-et-ratio.pdf.

Lambert, Michael. "Should We Be Teaching Children About Happiness in Schools?" Accessed October 24, 2017, http://www.thenational.ae/opinion/should-we-be-teaching-children-about-happiness-in-schools.

Liguori, Alphonsus. "On the Utility and Necessity of Prohibiting Harmful Books." Accessed October 24, 2017, https://thejosias.com/2015/07/22/on-the-utility-and-necessity-of-prohibiting-harmful-books.

Mark, Olwyn. "Passing on Faith." Accessed October 23, 2017. http://www.theosthinktank.co.uk/publications/2016/10/31/passing-on-faith.

Newman, John Henry. *Meditations on Christian Doctrine.* Accessed October 25, 2017. http://www.newmanreader.org/works/meditations/meditations9.html.

Ofcom. "Children and Parents: Media Use and Attitudes Report." Accessed October 24, 2017. https://www.ofcom.org.uk/__data/assets/pdf_file/0034/93976/Children-Parents-Media-Use-Attitudes-Report-2016.pdf.

Orwell, George. "Review of The Pub and The People by Mass-Observation." Accessed October 24, 2017. https://www.orwellfou

ndation.com/the-orwell-foundation/orwell/essays-and-other-wo
rks/review-of-the-pub-and-the-people-by-mass-observation.

Paul VI. *Populorum Progressio*. Accessed October 25, 2017. http://
w2.vatican.va/content/paul-vi/en/encyclicals/documents/hf_p-
vi_enc_26031967_populorum.html Populorum Progressio.

Peachey, Roy. "Fishing for Koi with an Afghan Veteran." Accessed
October 24, 2017. https://www.firstthings.com/web-exclusives/
2017/03/fishing-for-koi-with-an-afghan-veteran.

Richtel, Matt. "A Silicon Valley School That Doesn't Compute."
Accessed October 24, 2017, http://www.nytimes.com/2011/10/23
/technology/at-waldorf-school-in-silicon-valley-technology-can-
wait.html.

Seldon, Anthony. "Lessons in Life: Why I'm Teaching Happiness."
Accessed October 24, 2017, http://www.independent.co.uk/news
/education/education-news/lessons-in-life-why-im-teaching-hap
piness-6103354.html.

Shi, Rui, Shilei Zhang, and Danmin Miao. "Failure-Related Action
Orientation and Life Satisfaction: The Mediating Role of Forgivingness." *Journal of Happiness Studies* Vol. 17, Issue 5 (October
2016): 1891-1903. https://doi.org/10.1007/s10902-015-9676-y.

Taylor, Matthew. "Good Work: the Taylor Review of Modern Working Practices." Accessed October 26, 2017. https://www.gov.uk/
government/publications/good-work-the-taylor-review-of-mod-
ern-working-practices.

Waldstein, Edmund. "Contrasting Concepts of Freedom." Accessed
October 26, 2017. https://thejosias.com/2016/11/11/contrasting-
concepts-of-freedom.

Wired. "Steve Jobs: A Wired Life—The next insanely great thing."
Accessed October 24, 2017. http://www.wired.co.uk/article/the-
next-insanely-great-thing.